COWLEY PUBLICATIONS is a ministry of the brothers of the Society of Saint John the Evangelist, a monastic order in the Episcopal Church. Our mission is to provide books and resources for those seeking spiritual and theological formation. COWLEY PUBLICATIONS is committed to developing a new generation of writers and teachers who will encourage people to think and pray in new ways about spirituality, reconciliation, and the future.

To my beloved
friend, Nan...

I hope you and
your family have a
blessed, meaningful
and joyful Advent.

Love,
Pam

Awaiting the Child

AN ADVENT JOURNAL

Isabel Anders

COWLEY PUBLICATIONS

Cambridge, Massachusetts

Library of Congress Cataloging-in-Publication Data

Anders, Isabel, 1946–
    Awaiting the child : an Advent journal / Isabel Anders.
        p. cm.
    Includes bibliographical references.
    ISBN 1-56101-238-6 (pbk. : alk. paper) 1. Advent—Meditations.
2. Anders, Isabel, 1946– I. Title.
    BV40.A48 2005
    242'.33—dc22

Cover design: Rini Twait of Graphical Jazz, L.L.C.
Cover photo: Corbis Images
Interior design by Wendy Holdman

This book was printed in the United States of America on acid-free paper.

Cowley Publications
4 Brattle Street
Cambridge, Massachusetts 02138
800-225-1534 • www.cowley.org

To my daughters

. . . .

Contents

Preface to the New Edition

*W*ALLACE STEVENS WROTE that there is a poem at the heart of things. Advent is for me a season of longing to discover that "poem," that Golden Key that will unlock the mysteries of our being—our being here with each other—through the short days and the long nights.

The season of Advent offers us, each year, an opportunity to seek God within the geography of our souls—while living outwardly amid the roar and tumult of worldly events. How to find a synthesis? How to prepare a place of peace within—not only for ourselves, but for the good of all others?

This book was written as a search, guided by daily lectionary readings designated for the Advent season, as I contemplated, went about ordinary tasks, and compiled a journal during the early weeks of my first pregnancy. I reflected simply then that "writing is another way of allowing Christ to be born in and through me."

Madeleine L'Engle, who graciously wrote the introduction to the first edition of my book—encouraging a young writer to develop her voice—has said elsewhere that *nothing important is completely explicable.* That is certainly true of Advent and its sense of longing, its promise of a Coming, its demand for "active waiting" that stretches our selves to the limit. How to make room for God within?

As I look back on these pages, these chapters, I see

that many images of pain and glory—intricately particular and wide as the world, rich and faceted as jewels—came into play during the days and hours of that pivotal year in my life. Scripture scoops us up into the fray, but also sets us down in a place of birth, untidy and comforting as the manger, if we diligently take the Advent path.

I am still taking the journey, by God's grace, seeking to sniff out that poem that informs and undergirds my Christian life. As I have had the experience of living into maturity, and of writing other books, it has grown in me like a narrative of the soul, through subsequent years and events and life changes—even cataclysms—gathering up images and testing my mettle and enlarging me within.

And the central image of incarnation around which this book is built, that of the Child who *unto us is born,* remains core—it still burns with intensity and urgency for us in a world that desperately needs to acknowledge God With Us.

The image of Mary in her pregnancy, the Child "embedded" in her womb for the life of the world, is a picture of True Truth, an icon of hope for all humanity. It reminds us still, as it poignantly taught me then, that *our life is hid with Christ in God.*

New theories about the universe can certainly be seen to support this understanding, that in God we live and move and have our being. British biochemist Arthur Peacocke suggests that "we are that part of the cosmos consciously capable of being aware of and of responding to that immanent Presence."

And so *Awaiting the Child* is a call to awareness, as we all revisit the season of Advent and find it a new vista each time, yet also a marking-spot in the universe as familiar as our own hand—recalling G. K. Chesterton's illustration of sailing around the world in search of the meaning of life and returning to find it in the very place where he began.

Re-presenting *Awaiting the Child* in this new edition is a return for me, with gratitude and awe, hopes and prayers that it may serve as a map, a guide, an approach that, among other aids and offerings of this season, simply and surely points to Christ.

Introduction

I SABEL ANDERS WROTE these Advent meditations while waiting for her first baby to be born. I read them in my husband's hospital room, watching him die. Now another Advent approaches, another time when birth and death draw close together and it is not always possible to tell which is which.

As we move into Advent we are called to listen, something we seldom take time to do in this frenetic world of overactivity. But waiting for birth, waiting for death— these are listening times, when the normal distractions of life have lost their power to take us away from God's call to center in Christ.

Awaiting the Child is written to be read slowly, to be sipped, savored. Read a few lines and pause to think, to meditate on where our response is as the word touches our own lives. The life of a pregnant woman is focused on the amazing happenings of her body, the first faint flutterings of life, the stronger stirrings and kickings as the hidden infant grows. Isabel Anders quotes Coventry Patmore's description of the Virgin's womb and what goes on within: "The narrowness of that dwelling, the darkness, the mode of nourishment; He could not hear nor see, nor taste, nor move; He lay at all times fixed and bound; And by that rapture of captivity He set us free."

Free for the rapturous activity of enclosing a new life,

still invisible, a strange captivity which is a great blessing. The stranger captivity of watching a beloved spouse move out of his terrible captivity into God's love. How seldom are we able to comprehend the freedom of captivity!

During Advent we are traditionally called to contemplate death, judgment, hell, and heaven. To give birth to a baby is also a kind of death—death to the incredible intimacy of carrying a child, death to old ways of life and birth into new—and it is as strange for the parents as for the baby. Judgment: John of the Cross says that in the evening of life we shall be judged on love; not on our accomplishments, not on our successes and failures in the worldly sense, but solely on love.

If a woman resents the entire process of childbearing, then she is already in hell. If she rejoices in the extraordinary mystery of bearing a child conceived in love, then she already tastes heaven. Often we identify with Mary, and Mary's incredible courage and love inform ours.

"Narrowing down, focusing in," Isabel Anders continues, "has something to do with identifying with our Lord in his first coming." What an appropriate thought for a woman, narrowing down, focusing in on the approaching birth of a baby. But this is not a book merely for pregnant women or even for women in general. I, too, my hand in my husband's, am narrowing down, focusing in, for this narrowing down is on the Second Coming of Christ, that time of the healing of the universe when all will be understood, even what is incomprehensible to me now—the inexorable dying of a man I have lived with and loved for forty years.

The baby Isabel Anders is carrying will leave her in a different way; first it will leave the intimacy of the womb, then of the breast. Ultimately the child grows into an adult and leaves home; we experience death and birth over and over.

Isabel Anders points out that it is not easy to keep a listening Advent in our consumer culture, with Christmas decorations going up in shop windows and on the streets even before Thanksgiving, with trees undressed and put out for garbage the day after Christmas. "In silence, in hiddenness," she writes, "the seed of our hope is nurtured—our belief that Christ has come, does come, and will come. What Advent means day to day will be different for each of us."

Through these meditations her own belief shines with a quiet and steady light, a belief that I have witnessed moving quietly to an ever more and more flexible view of God's love as she has moved through the deaths and births of her own life.

Anders points out that Advent can be seen as a triptych, when chronological time opens up and we can see simultaneously Christ's "earthly coming to a manger in Bethlehem; his coming to each of us by faith in our hearts; and the anticipation of the future Day of the Lord: his coming again in glory."

Once again, as happened during the past nearly two thousand years, predictions are being made of the time of this Second Coming, which, Jesus emphasized, "even the angels in heaven do not know." But we human creatures, who are "a little lower than the angels," too frequently try to set ourselves above them with our predictions and our arrogant assumption of a knowledge which God hid even from angels. Advent is not a time to declare, but to listen, to listen to whatever God may want to tell us through the singing of the stars, the quickening of a baby, the gallantry of a dying man.

Listen. Quietly. Humbly. Without arrogance.

It horrifies me that not a few Christians are equating the Second Coming with nuclear destruction. They believe that they will see Christ coming riding on a mushroom cloud in triumph. They, of course, will be raptured, wafted off to heaven, untouched either bodily or spiritually by the pain and burning and devastation of all those around them.

Thank God there is no hint of this self-centered and hard-hearted thinking in Isabel Anders's book. She sees the promise of God's coming in glory in the words of the Old Testament prophets, who tell us that "we have erred, gone our way—but One will come to make all right. All creation [*all* creation, mind you, not just our planet, or a small segment of our planet's population] longs for that day when God alone will be exalted." Then our understanding of the incarnation will be made clear.

She quotes from the Syrian liturgy of St. James: "Thou hast united, O Lord, thy divinity with our humanity and our humanity with thy divinity, thy life with our mortality and our mortality with thy life. Thou hast received what was ours and given unto us what was thine."

How these thoughts enrich and ennoble birth and death!

In the first verse of "Jesu, Joy of Man's Desiring," we sing, "Word of God, our flesh that fashioned with the fire of life impassioned," and the marvelous mystery of incarnation shines. "Because in the mystery of the Word made flesh," goes one of my favorite propers, for it is indeed the mystery by which we live, give birth, watch death.

When the Second Person of the Trinity entered the Virgin's womb and prepared to be born as a human baby (a particular baby, Jesus of Nazareth), his death was inevitable; all we human beings who are born also ultimately die. All of us at one time or another act outside the ways of love, and when we do this we must repent of our lack of love.

John the Baptist called us to repent, and Isabel Anders points out that "the call to repentance must always precede praise." And it must always be followed by praise. After we have asked for forgiveness of our sins, then we must accept that forgiveness and respond to that acceptance with a great cry of thanksgiving.

"Writing this journal," Isabel Anders says, and surely it is true for all of us journal-writers, "is a quiet performance in the privacy of my world, as I fit it into the rest of my ordered life. . . . There is a hiddenness to my work on these pages, not so different from the interiority of a child being formed inside its mother." She talks about the inevitability of delays, even harsh rejections, when one sends writing out to publishers.

She continues, "I find the pain of delay is not alien to Advent thinking," adding that "it is a risk, nevertheless, to write and publish, to put it all out for display and judgment." But isn't it similar in its own small way to the risk Jesus took in being born? "Writing is another way of allowing Christ to be born in and through me." Yes. I, too, have referred to the artist, male as well as female, as being like Mary, in being willing to be impregnated by the Holy Spirit.

It is only after we have been enabled to say, "Be it unto me according to your Word," that we can accept the paradoxes of Christianity. Christ comes to live with us, bringing an incredible promise of God's love; but never are we promised that there will be no pain, no suffering, no death, but rather that these very griefs are the road to love and eternal life.

Isabel Anders contrasts "summery spirituality" with "wintry spirituality," and, like her, I tend to identify with the wintry view. She writes: "No summer day is ever without a reminder that this is not the condition one can expect of the whole year. . . . When all of life is too light, too full, we may be deceived into thinking we deserve its benefits and comforts. Winter does not allow us that option. . . . Wintry spirituality is a kind of awareness, an acceptance of paradox, the coexistence of the irreconcilable. . . . To emerge from the winter of the soul as still oneself, is to affirm the permanent goodness of creation, to validate life as it has been given. Though life is never again the same, yet it is wholly renewed."

Strangely I have found in my own life that it is only through a wintry spirituality that I am able to affirm summer and sunshine. A friend wrote me recently, "Winter reveals structure." Only as the structure is firmly there are we able to dress it with the lovely trappings of spring, budding leaves, rosy blossoms. Winter is the quiet, fallow time when the earth prepares for the rebirth of spring. Unless the seed is put into the ground to die, it cannot be born.

In her last meditation Isabel Anders writes: "It is Christmas Eve and the paradox stands. . . . Christ's coming is both a cosmic revealing and a hidden thing. . . . God is known to us in paradox, in flesh and in spirit."

In Advent we prepare for the coming of all Love, that love which will redeem all the brokenness, wrongness, hardnesses of heart which have afflicted us.

Awaiting the Child is lovingly written, and my response as I read it was an inner warmth as my own love was rekindled.

Madeleine L'Engle
Advent 1986

Advent One

Almighty God, give us grace to cast away the works of darkness, and put on the armor of light, now in the time of this mortal life in which your Son Jesus Christ came to visit us in great humility; that in the last day, when he shall come again in his glorious majesty to judge both the living and the dead, we may rise to the life immortal; through him who lives and reigns with you and the Holy Spirit, one God, now and for ever.

Narrowing Down

For salvation is nearer to us now than when we became believers; the night is far gone, the day is near.

$\mathcal{A}$DVENT IS A TIME of narrowing down, focusing in. I feel its coming in my bones, with the inevitability of the shorter, darkening days. Our worship too takes on the character of the season—not somber, but sober. It is a time of reflection and quiet seriousness, not of frivolity.

For me, this Advent includes a narrowing down of another kind. I am at home rather than in an office—still working as an editor and writer, but fewer hours, and in more solitude. For a number of years I worked full time in publishing, an eight-hour day. I could be reached by phone in a specific office, fulfilling a specific role. Life within the busy network of departments had many variables, and I was surrounded by constant activity.

Since my husband, an Episcopal priest, and I were called to this parish church, I am too far away to commute to the office daily. So my work sphere has become smaller—an upstairs study, a phone, but much less stimulation and a more isolated circumstance.

For the time being it is enjoyable, a kind of rest from

the hectic pace I had kept. Narrowing down to this house, this office, this work before me, is a choice as well as a necessity. It is good to be here—not as an escape from the world, but as a chance for a new perspective on the world I am still related to: that of editing and publishing. I find the narrowness leaves me fewer choices, yet somehow more space to be at home in. Not having to commute also gives me more time to read, write, and reflect—activities that are important to me, and are especially related to Advent.

We came here by choice, agreeing to accept the call to minister to these particular people, in this place. Although the call was extended in fact only to my husband, every aspect of it affects me, too. I am operating from a different center, spending my time in the company of and sharing worship with new people. But together my husband and I agreed to these changes, accepting placement to a spot on the Chicago map we had never explored before. Through a series of circumstances this neighborhood became our home, these people our church family, and this rectory our center.

We are adjusting to all the changes. Phones now ring for us here. We are available, and that is part of our focusing in. I cannot travel as much, or touch as many points, or fulfill as many tasks as I could when I was a full-time office worker. But my dual life as both worker and wife is clear and the two are quite compatible.

An engraved door knocker with our names upon it, received as a wedding gift, now graces this doorway and identifies us as belonging in this house, at this address. Small details signal this narrowing down, focusing in.

A circle is already beginning to grow around this center,

this home as a focus for ministry. We experience the vitality of joining a new worshiping community, with its power to draw others into its circumference. As my husband has been calling on homes of lapsed or irregularly attending parishioners—some who haven't come for years—many have already responded. There is a rightness to their reclaiming their church home as they enter its doors again.

We are a small and varied group who gather in a neighborhood church to meet, to worship God in word and sacrament. We occupy ourselves also as stewards of the gifts of land and properties, caring for their beauty and efficiency, tending the buildings that enable us to gather. Thus we hallow and respect places and things with a true Anglican concern that is, we hope, midway between "superstition and slovenliness," in the words of poet George Herbert.

Our concern for details constitutes a narrowing down, a focusing on the essentials—heat to stave off the increasing cold, care for the maintenance and improvement of the material gifts we have inherited in this place. The spirit of narrowing down prepares us also for the work of inner maintenance that is part of Advent discipline.

Why concern ourselves with a limited plot of earth, one small parish, a few people who may never "appreciate" us or enhance our image? Why limit ourselves in such a commitment when the whole world is open to be conquered—and growth and expansion are the valued words in our culture? Yet without some vision of the value of individual souls, some hope for growth and fruition of ministry down the months and years, it would seem absurd to work so hard at plans or programs, or to listen to individual problems hours on end ... or to be part of a handful of worshipers at a weeknight service, faithfully gathering, week after week, to hear the words of a liturgy that points us beyond ourselves and our limited lives.

Who is listening to our voices, and who cares? What difference would it make if we were, instead, to spend our time building up our own fame and fortune? Would it upset some balance of good if this neighborhood no longer harbored such a group of people worshiping inside these stone walls? Can we have faith that our prayers penetrate them and extend beyond our borders?

Underlying all our doubt is a belief that our limitations, our narrowing down, do have a purpose. In Advent we affirm that the greatest things can take place in small, enclosed spaces. In the words of Coventry Patmore,

> "The Virgin's womb." The narrowness of that
> dwelling, the darkness, the mode of nourishment;
> He could not hear, nor see, nor taste, nor move;
> He lay at all times fixed and bound;
> > And by that rapture of captivity
> > He made us free
> > His blissful prisoners likewise to be.

Narrowing down, focusing in, has something to do with identifying with our Lord in his first coming. Our worship is a response to the mystery of limitation for a purpose. We believe that to forget God is to forget ourselves, our nature, and our relationship to God. We neglect to praise, decline to enter the mystery, at our own peril. It takes such a short lapse to begin to forget altogether.

Scripture passages in Advent particularly remind us that we must narrow down in order to do something; there is an urgency, for "the night is far gone, the day is near" (Rom. 13:12). Advent itself is a kind of night. When we enter this church season, we know by calculating the weeks exactly when daylight will emerge in its mid-winter splendor at the celebration of the Christ Mass. But we choose to forget, to put aside the realization of the coming light so that we may taste the darkness of night more fully, and wait for joy.

> For salvation is nearer to us now than when we became believers; . . . Let us then lay aside the works of darkness and put on the armor of light; let us live honorably as in the day, . . . not in debauchery and licentiousness, not in quarreling and jealousy. Instead, put on the Lord Jesus Christ, and make no provision for the flesh, to gratify its desires. (Rom. 13:11–14)

Because we have the peace of Christ within, we can step back from its full realization to await his coming anew, to our small circle of believers in this place. We limit our plans, while our devotional thoughts go inward.

Yet it is almost impossible to preserve any sense of keeping Advent in the culture about us. Many people are getting a jump on Christmas already, even before Thanksgiving has faded. Yet we look for a fine distinction here. We need not "mortify" ourselves—only watch, listen, and prepare. In silence, in hiddenness, the seed of our hope is nurtured—our belief that Christ has come, does come, and will come. What Advent means from day to day will be different for each of us; so will our experience of his coming.

For me this is a most unusual Advent, as I begin to await

the birth of our first child. This season marks the beginning of long months of waiting. It is a secret my husband and I are keeping to ourselves for now, but which we will share before long with our parish family.

So far, my thoughts about the baby surprise me. They are far more practical than emotional. I am planning carefully, thankful for the health to keep active, working. I am trying to conserve my strength in small ways, making careful decisions, slowly accommodating this new fact without becoming overwhelmed by its implications. It is such a welcome task for me to be narrowing down at this time.

In pregnancy there are limitations for a purpose, as in any work worth doing. I am thankful for the warmth of this home, the security of these walls. To be here is to know the joy of centering and focusing. The boundaries of my life, like these four walls, seem clear and desirable. "The boundary lines have fallen for me in pleasant places," says the Psalmist, and I can say the same.

So I commit these lines to this journal, in preparation for what I will discover in the days and weeks ahead. I pray for wisdom and for the grace to do what is necessary, put up with the limits to my activity and the narrowing of my priorities. I anticipate the thoughts and themes that the Advent cycle will provide for the strengthening of my mind and body and spirit.

The Tree

But it is not the spiritual that is first, but the physical,
and then the spiritual.

ODAY WAS MY FIRST visit to the doctor. He con-
firmed the pregnancy—and although I already knew,
somehow it made a difference. On his office walls are displayed pictures of all the babies he has delivered. When
I first entered and saw that sea of faces, I began to feel unexpectedly tearful. It was as though I had been given a startling reminder of what I was there for.

Suddenly I could imagine our baby's picture joining
that host, "like the stars of the sky." I imagined it not as
a baby (as we had been thinking in our minds) but as a
specific face, though yet unseen. Pulling myself together,
I went through the examination and everything checked
out fine. My husband was called in from the waiting room
and told, "You are going to be a father." I was given a little
book on prenatal care and some vitamins and was told to
use common sense in eating and activities.

The thought of faces as a host of stars reminds me of
the story of Abraham's promise from God, as he was about
to sacrifice his only son at God's command. Instead, God
at the last minute made provision for an animal sacrifice,

and promised that his progeny would flourish "as the stars" and "as the sand which is on the seashore" (Gen. 22:17).

All this natural imagery brings me back to one of the earliest pictures we come upon in the Bible—the Tree of Life in the garden of Eden. It is a mysterious, fleeting reference. The image of the tree is to recur repeatedly in the history of God's working through the generations.

Today, in the morning prayer office with my husband, we read Psalm 1,

> They are like trees
>> planted by streams of water,
> which yield their fruit in its season . . . (v. 3)

and I clearly remember Psalm 128, read at our wedding:

> Your wife will be like a fruitful vine
>> within your house;
> your children will be like olive shoots
>> around your table. (v. 3)

The Tree of Life, in God's plan, is more than a figure of speech. It is a description of the physical branching out of families, one way through which God's Word and ways may be passed on. In this context, parenthood is both the most natural of callings and the most humbling privilege.

It is important to remember how much God cares about physical life. For all my abstract thinking in images and ideas, my greatest task at the moment is to eat and drink properly to become a fit branch for the flowering of a new life. "It is not the spiritual that is first, but the physical, and then the spiritual," Paul reminds us in 1 Corinthians 15:46.

These images have been mostly spiritual to me through the years, lovely pictures, before I was in a position to contemplate parenthood. When it did become time, my old ways of thinking about "the tree" became livelier. One prays and hopes for "the blessing of children," but today's confirmation of my pregnancy comes as a wave of new possibility, of strength and assurance.

Perhaps it has been easy for me to see this tree imagery only as a metaphor because I have been so far from working with the earth, from cultivating the soil. My husband works in the garden, but I have never enjoyed it. I am amazed when I can keep a house plant blooming! I do love the hymn from the *Didache* that reminds us that the very bread of Eucharist is from an earthly source, the natural product of the planted, harvested, growing stalk, broken for us:

> As grain once scattered on the hillsides was in this
> broken bread made one
> So from all lands thy Church be gathered into thy
> kingdom by thy Son.

When Jesus taught the mysteries of his kingdom, he so often used the principle of physical growth and of paradox—as in the parable of the mustard seed, the smallest of all seeds, a mere pittance. Yet "when it has grown it is the greatest of shrubs and becomes a tree, so that the birds of the air come and make nests in its branches" (Matt. 13:32). The vision of that end product—the tree filled with birdsong—is a rich symbol of ongoing life, a motif of joy that brightens the natural world.

In "A Celibate Epiphany," poet Luci Shaw writes of God's early "planting" of the seed of humankind that was to flourish into redemption for the entire race. She carries the theme all the way back to Eve.

> His light shines,
> lingers,
> & all glories glance
> upon her inward parts.
> His purpose finds
> her heart of hearts,
> conceiving Jesus
> at her core
> by his most
> Holy Ghost. Once more,
> as with lonely Mary, he
> makes of her in her own time
> & in his time, his sweet
> bride, also a tree
> thick enough to climb
> with petals
> for the eye's delight
> & fruit to eat.

As the foreshadowing of Jesus' conception began with the first woman, and the promise was brought to fruition in Mary, so that tree, built through generations out of the root of Jesse, is truly a Tree of Life, nurtured in the most human manner. Earthly lives and deaths are its tenuous branches, faithfulness and weakness are woven into its life, and God calls blessed those who choose to "abide" in love in order to bear the necessary fruit.

Human life, it seems, is never irrelevant to God's plan. Instead, we are in the thick of it. We can enter into this design, this story, by accepting the joys and pains of our humanity and submitting them to the good of the kingdom. We can rejoice that participation in its growth is allowed, and cooperate by choosing those things that build and sustain life for our families, our communities, our world. As Moses urged his people Israel in the crucial early stages of the tree's growth: "Choose life so that you and your descendants may live" (Deut. 30:19).

The branches of the kingdom spread out today, "thick enough to climb"; and in human life we find the joys of communion and pleasures of fulfillment—such as parenthood—grow along with it.

Growth, whether physical or spiritual, is never without some stretching, some pain. I want to reaffirm my choice to submit to this necessity as the weeks and months progress, to understand it as a privilege, part of my participation in the kingdom. Learning about the stages of our child's growth helps me to feel more connected with the design of the Creator and to appreciate the fact that God sustains and replenishes life in the natural world around us.

The tree has been a symbol of life from the very beginning. But we cannot forget that in the sweep of the continuing story, life and death converged on a tree—the cross of wood that both took Christ's earthly life and won our redemption into ongoing life.

As the seed for the tree begins as a very small entity, yet

carries in it all the potential for the flowering of the whole tree, so Advent carries in it the seed of the whole drama of our salvation. The planting, the watering, the tending can be conscious acts in our lives, as we wait for God to give the increase, to bring about these purposes in the world and in our lives—in this place, in this hour.

Welcome, All Wonders!

Welcome, all wonders in one sight!
Eternity shut in a span.

*I*N THIS SEASON we celebrate on three levels the coming of the Lord. We remember his earthly coming to
a manger in Bethlehem, we celebrate his coming to each
of us by faith in our hearts ("How silently, how silently the
wondrous gift is given"), and we anticipate the future Day
of the Lord: his coming again in glory. We are asked to
contemplate his advent on all three levels simultaneously.
One way we might imagine this is to think of a medieval
painting, a triptych, in which three completely different
scenes are visible at once. In such a view eternity meets in
our hearts, in the world, in Christ.

Seventeenth-century English poet Richard Crashaw
makes artful music of this paradox in his "Nativity Hymn,"
rendering it almost visual:

> Welcome, all wonders in one sight!
> > Eternity shut in a span,
> Summer in winter, day in night,
> > Heaven in earth and God in man!
> Great little one! whose all-embracing birth
> > Lifts earth to heaven, stoops heaven to earth.

It is primarily in worship, in the liturgy, that we are able in a mystery to touch each of these bases and embrace these facets of his coming. In the language of praise, we are not forced to define the advent of Jesus in only one way.

In the first panel of this triptych we rely on the gospel accounts of an actual physical birth, in hardship and meager circumstances. The more we are able to return to the humanness of that scene, through identifying with Mary in the labor of birth, with Joseph in his efforts to protect and preserve, the less apt we will be to idealize it, to cover it with gold leaf and jewels as an artist might gild the icon of the cross, in order to hide its awful reality. The first scene makes concrete the other two understandings of Christ's coming because it puts him in the thick of things, within our history and our world.

The second panel of our painting is as particular as the individual, who can only approach the mystery of God breaking through and "coming" to her in her actual time and specific circumstances.

Here is such a circumstance: Today I am driving on icy expressways in bumper-to-bumper traffic along with lines of trucks, pondering the Scripture lessons of the season. I do battle with perilous ice patches, a dirty windshield, and the frustrations of a twenty-minute delay to my editorial office twenty-five miles away. Only the manuscripts in my briefcase, ready to turn in, give purpose to my struggles. I do experience a sense of completion as I bring in the work I have done, and feel gratitude for this connection with the whole process of publishing—even when I must travel on days like this.

I wish I had thought to bring some tapes of Advent

carols, some of my favorite music, to play on the car's tape player in order to lift my spirit above the grime.

I need to hear again the themes of God's love, Christ's coming—to realize that the journey to Bethlehem to be taxed and numbered must have been no picnic either. For me, these mundane conditions are also a scenario of Christ's coming into my life—with meaning and unlikely hope. It is folly to think that if we only had perfect, even different circumstances, it would be easy to see Christ's entrance into the world. It is never easy to believe that God will come to us. We probably think it was clearer to those Old Testament saints who saw burning bushes and heard majestic voices. Perhaps the world of nature and supernature seemed much more alive to people then—without traffic noise and stereo static to interfere.

Yet they had a different hindrance. Nature said too many things that were beyond their understanding of causes; it had too many voices, which now we call "natural occurrences." Today we think we have the visible physical world pretty well figured out, so we tend to miss God's voice. The task of the ancients was different; they had to discover *whose* voice they were hearing, discern what god was breaking through. Many today, perhaps all but a remnant, have ceased to believe in God's breaking through at all.

My own scenario of Christ's coming here and now is ongoing, not finished. I want to see his kingdom coming in small ways, in the unfolding of days, in the completion of tasks . . . right now in the transfer of these manuscripts that helps our editorial department keep on schedule and may mean an author's book will be produced in time for a fall convention.

It all matters. The world is full of more than myself and my concerns. Acknowledging the broadness of Christ's coming reminds me that I am just one link, part of only one scene; what I do matters, but not in any paramount sense. Each person on this expressway has some task and is connected to others by a network of responsibilities and concerns. All of them I must see as people for whom Christ came, and is coming.

Are they prepared to hear his voice breaking through, against all odds? Advent is surely one of the hardest times of the year to explain, even among church people. Do they know what the season is, or do the early Christmas lights and increased traffic downtown make them weary of the whole thing already? Are they broke, and dreading the financial demands of the approaching holiday? Have they ever truly connected Christ with his mass at Christmas?

It is hard and costly to accept that Christ has come and is coming and will come.

Christ *will* come. The third panel of this triptych is the most mysterious and the hardest of all to grasp. Even as we strain to believe in his coming, to understand the concept, we must rely heavily on the veiled words of biblical imagery: of the king reigning in Zion on his holy hill, the Alpha and the Omega, the Supper of the Lamb. Jumping from our concrete and ordinary lives to envision, even fleetingly, a consummation of our hopes, a final triumph of our God over evil, is always more than we can handle. Again, we depend on the language and tradition of Christian worship to bridge the gap, to stretch our imaginations, even as they give us something to do with our bodies: to kneel, to praise in song, to commune with each other sacramentally.

Even so, how are we to make way, to prepare actively

for what we believe will occur "in the fullness of time"? Perhaps one way is to reflect on these themes of Advent seriously: God in flesh in a manger; darkness turning to light; a banquet; a wedding. . . . What a task, to try to hold these three separate scenes together, these three levels of expectation, in a cutaway picture of Christian hope.

In this season I seek to embrace this image, welcoming "all wonders in one sight." One way to work on this is to meditate on the passages of Scripture designated for these days and weeks of Advent.

As I live through my own scenes day by day, I hope to be able to make connections between Word and experience, to hold the truth of Christ's coming beneath the demands and fulfillments of the day, an unspoken prayer and belief. Even when some portion of the vision fades for a while, and I slip into doubt, I can return to these images as traces in a mirror. *Lord, I believe; help my unbelief.*

Even now the fact of his comings—past, present, and future—imperceptibly "lifts earth to heaven, stoops heaven to earth."

Active Waiting

It is Christ the Lord who is everlastingly in the world reconciling it to God, and it is he who acts through a faithful human agent whenever, by the power of agape, *one soul lovingly invades another.*

TODAY I AM WAITING for the mail, as usual, with the expectation not only of some personal correspondence, but also of word from several publishers, further instructions on some writing assignments, and payment for work already completed. Usually I find that I do not receive the thing I expect on a given day, but often some totally unthought-of person writes to ask me to do an article, sends a book for me to review, or responds to something I've published—usually those who bother to do so have something favorable to say.

Expectation is a large part of my life as I work at home: waiting for the mail or the phone to interrupt the work I'm doing, to nudge me onto another track. Such breaks usually refresh me, but sometimes they throw me off and distract me, making the next hour or so almost useless. But without the outside world breaking in—my husband offering to meet me for lunch, a parishioner just wanting to talk—my day is almost too serene, and can also be *static* when I'm by myself and have no interpersonal interaction.

The practice of waiting fits into my life comfortably; it is not a new or startling theme, but a familiar strain. It is ingrained in me from years of meditating on those Psalms and Proverbs that urge us to wait on the Lord while going about our lives of service, to remain expectant while continuing to complete the tasks before us. Active waiting is not only one of the paradoxes of Advent, but actually a way of life recommended for Christians at any time. C. S. Lewis described it as living day to day with a kind of cheerful insecurity.

In Hebrew thought, reflected especially in the Old Testament wisdom writings, waiting is seen to be an occupation, a way of life—not a passive stance or, least of all, an excuse for inaction. In Psalm 25, appointed for Advent, I read, "Lead me in your truth, and teach me, for you are the God of my salvation; for you I wait all day long."

The day *is* long, but waiting is not meant to fill its hours so much as to characterize one aspect of the complex human reaction we have to events and circumstances. Such waiting is a readiness to respond not only to mail and telephones, as in my case, but to God's breaking in through other people to stir us to action.

It is foolishness to talk of waiting at all unless there is Someone to wait for. In Hebrew thinking the assumption is always that God *is*, the great I AM. Ours is an I–Thou situation in which dialogue is possible; communication goes on between heaven and earth, the channels are open, and how we respond and what we do here matters.

Waiting would be utter folly and waste were it not based on the nature of God and God's desire to act on our behalf. Waiting is right for us because God is the Creator, the Lord from heaven who enters our earthly story, as we acknowledge especially in this season.

We believe that God will not leave us waiting forever. There is a linear connection between God's works in history past and history present up to our own day. In looking back we can see the evidence of God's abiding presence. Just as a line of faithful people, a continuous genealogy, brought Christ to earth, joined to the human family through Mary—we too are connected to God's acts in the future through our waiting and preparing our hearts for Christ's coming again. We have not yet seen all that our Lord will do—yet we believe.

Our will becomes conformed to God's as we are faithful day by day and choose to allow God to dwell in us, breathe through us, and mold our lives. This is what the British novelist and theologian Charles Williams refers to as "in-othering," truly loving our neighbor as ourself; and "in-Godding," being incorporated into Christ through redemption. Both are part of the divine plan for humankind, begun at creation, wrought by Christ, insured in resurrection. Together, in-othering and in-Godding constitute a way of living in which we can choose to participate by our daily actions.

Carroll E. Simcox refers to this process most accurately:

> The "othering" of one's self involves a radical and total self-identification with the other in what is, in fact, a manifestation of Christ's saving incarnation. It is Christ the Lord who is everlastingly in the world reconciling it to God, and it is he who

acts through a faithful human agent whenever,
by the power of *agape,* one soul lovingly invades
another.

This process of in-othering truly is the action of agape,
and is reflective of and draws from the power of Christ's
own self-identification with us in our humanity, in order
to redeem that which he assumed—flesh itself. He spent
thirty years of his life waiting, not taking charge as one
would expect a king to do, but eating and drinking, living
and working among ordinary folk and being known as a
son, brother, friend, and teacher in one specific place. Active
waiting characterized his life until the "fullness of time"
when he began to be revealed—to a few—as Messiah.

He assumed flesh, living within its limitations, and thus
brought men and women into God. And the amazing reality of his life and work serves as an example for us as well.
The in-othering begins here on earth, through the least
likely means of living humanly day by day. We participate
in it by allowing God's Spirit to fill us more and more
until God permeates our lives, our hopes, our very quality
of existence. "All the way to heaven is heaven," said Saint
Teresa. We are meant to experience a quality of spiritual
life here that reflects our being on the way to heaven.

Barbara Reynolds, one translator of Dante's *Paradise,*
and a former professor of mine, writes in her introduction:

It has been said [by C. S. Lewis] that the joys of
heaven would be for most of us, in our present condition, an acquired taste. In a sense, Dante's *Paradise*
is a story about the acquisition of that taste.

Active waiting, too, may be said to be a gradual acquisition of that taste. If we could for a moment see the cosmic implications of our waiting with and for God, we would be astonished at the glory of "ordinary" things in our lives, and the significance of other people.

All of our actions either affirm or deny God's image in others. C. S. Lewis writes, "All day long we are . . . helping each other to one or other of these destinations"—meaning heaven or hell. "There are no ordinary people," he continues. "You have never talked to a mere mortal. . . . It is immortals whom we joke with, work with, marry, snub, and exploit—immortal horrors or everlasting splendours."

The reality of the in-othering Lewis and Simcox speak of has never seemed more real to me than in this pregnancy, when I actually carry around with me another person who has "lovingly invaded" me. Or is it the other way around? This overlapping of my destiny with the well-being of my child is a new thing, and I am acutely aware that everything I do affects the future of another person. It is bearable because my life, and the baby's life, are "hid with Christ in God." The in-Godding starts here and now, in this time of active waiting.

Amid this metaphysical understanding I find myself living, eating, drinking, resting, and caring for my body in simple ways that are as much my Christian duty as any mental or spiritual work has ever been. I am aware of being on a journey within my own soul, one that will be forever life-changing as it leads me to the task and vocation of parenthood. It is a time of active waiting that prepares me for new lessons in loving, as I approach the miracle of birth—a gift of God, quite beyond my control or credit.

I want to take the remaining months of this journey

with as much awareness and preparation as possible, physically and spiritually. The process of waiting is already changing my husband and me. We are living with the fact that we can't see what we know is happening inside my womb, or measure it very accurately; we have heard only the wonderful sound of the baby's heartbeat, amplified by the doctor's instrument set on my stomach. Trusting God for the outcome of this pregnancy is a strong reminder that our humanity has its limits—sometimes very humbling ones. We have elected not to have any extraordinary tests done as long as things progress normally. We are praying without seeking any special reassurances.

The activity in this period of waiting is subtle: Already my focus is shifting from only myself, my husband, work, church, and friends to include a new responsibility and a coming joy: a new life. Patience and acceptance are ways for me, at this point in my life, to agree to the in-othering and the in-Godding.

Lord, give grace in these days and those to come as we wait actively for the in-Godding—for your coming in our lives.

Journey into Light

The Truth must dazzle gradually
or every man be blind—

*T*HE WORLD SEEMS brighter today—or perhaps I am getting more used to the grayness. Darkness is increasingly sapping the daylight hours as we head down to the shortest day of the year, December 21. But at that lowest point we also begin to rise, with the days, toward a new beginning.

Here is one of the paradoxes of Advent, which also reflects our hope—our belief that God is working in the night as though it were already day. Psalm 139 says of the Lord: "Even the darkness is not dark to you; the night is as bright as the day, for darkness is as light to you" (v. 12).

Yet because we are human, it is never easy for us to remember the light when we are in darkness. And it is hard to believe in the power of light when it does not manifest itself to our eyes. The Christian calendar helps us to tread the same path that others have followed through the years, knowing intuitively what will come next and believing that joy comes through waiting, that reward follows discipline.

There is a sense of urgency in the darkness that we do not feel in the light. The days themselves help us, keep us active. The work that we have been given to do presses us on. We have fewer daylight hours in which to see the dust to remove it, less time to travel in hours blessed by the sun. Of necessity we work around what nature provides us, adjusting ourselves to the reality of winter.

In this part of the country, in Chicago, we become indoor creatures for survival. We add warm layers of woolens and fleeces. We burrow in—psychologically, perhaps, as well as physically. But spiritually? It is a challenge most of all to our spirits to fight the pull of impending darkness each afternoon, not to call the day over, or to fear that the night itself is far spent. Isn't loneliness greater this time of year, when we are all supposed to be filled with anticipation and warmth in the glow of family times and celebrations?

Perhaps we need the lights of Advent, the colors, the trees and candles and customs we follow, the green of evergreen branches, the Jesse tree with its many-colored symbols, to bring a reminder of hope and light into our midwinter bleakness, our loneliness and longing for day. It is human to desire and share signs of hope in these tangible ways, and the symbols of our faith can mean more to us when they are spare and carefully chosen for the season, rather than overdone or too celebrative.

In our church tradition Advent is seen as a time of reflection and preparation for Christmas joy, while in the general culture most people think of the first twenty-four days of December as part of the celebration itself. It is very hard to hold to a discipline of study and prayer, waiting and planning, when the world around us is doing another thing entirely.

The Great Litany that introduced our worship last Sunday helped to set a mood of "first things first." Imploring

God's mercy and deliverance, and bringing before God the ills and needs of our time, helps us get a perspective on what Advent is meant to be, and how unusual a season it is to occur in the midst of the world's heaviest buying spree.

Our worship reminds us that spiritually we are beginning a journey from relative darkness into the light of Christ for our lives, in this year of our Lord. Last Sunday purple vestments gave a suggestion of both penitence and kingship. Above was hanging our traditional Advent wreath with one purple candle lit, a lonely promise of more force and light to come. The children came forward at the end to light their own small wreath, and my husband talked about its meaning, of which we all needed reminding.

We will light one candle each week in Advent, and the circumference of light will grow even as the darkness increases in the world outside, week by week. We are, no less than the ancients, holding off the darkness. Yet we do it not in ignorance or fear, but in deliberate commemoration of this season of hope and preparation. Our lights are offered to God as a prayer: "Stir up your power, O Lord, and with great might come among us." And as we pray, our hopes grow with the light.

I feel the richness of our calendar especially at this time when prophets, shepherds, and angels all have already taken part in the story that is unfolding. We as worshipers are joining them, through reading aloud the message, proclaiming it in acts of ministry, and calling Christ our hope through the shared communion of his table each week.

I ponder the meaning of the candles, seeking a focus for each one. People vary in their interpretations of the significance of each week and its candle—three purple and one pink. The names of Isaiah and the other prophets, John the Baptist, and Mary the mother of Jesus are very much intertwined in our remembrance of the events that led up to Christ's birth in that first Advent. The third Sunday of Advent, when the pink candle is lighted, marks a slight break in mood, a lightening of tone along with the variation in color; then the fourth Sunday, with its purple again, reminds us that only a few days remain until we celebrate the lighting of the white Christ candle in the center and complete the symbol, surrounding its purpose in light.

In the circle of the Advent wreath we are reminded that our church year is not only cyclical, but historical and yet still unfolding—as readings in the life of the nation Israel and the events leading up to Christ's birth are connected to the custom of the lightings. The paradox of change and repetition is also part of our worship life in any season, as we bring recollections of other Advents, other seasons of the church year along with us to *this* moment. Yet we also expect our journey into light to be different this year, as the circumstances of our lives are different. We are prepared for it to reveal a new inner landscape and bring us into fresh understanding as we are touched by the light.

I have read that the Advent wreath itself is derived from an ancient rite among tribes of northern Europe. It was customary, in those countries where the winter days are even shorter than ours and the nights rule, to try to reclaim something of the light when the sun seemed to be hiding itself from the earth. It is said that the first such wreaths were made of wagon wheels decorated with evergreens and candles and hung up in homes as a symbol of hope. The shape and general custom was later adopted by Christians to represent in a dramatic way the progression of the weeks before Christmas, illuminating the darkness of a world waiting for Christ. The fully lit wreath displays a brilliance that seems to merge in our minds with the revealing light of the star over Bethlehem—a light to lighten the Gentiles, and a sign to God's people, Israel.

It is wise and helpful to know what we are commemorating, in order to bring our intellects to reflect upon the seemingly primitive rituals of the season. We cannot rush the coming of the light with our impatience or even our zeal. God can wait—did wait—to send Christ. And we must wait: through the shifting light and darkness of these days, and of our fortunes.

We wait as the world did in Christ's day, and in all ages of oppression, for deliverance from the darkness of our sins and weaknesses, our negligence, our lack of belief. Even the merest flickering candle can serve to remind us that the Lord is still God. This is what we proclaim in the liturgy, sometimes weakly, yet reflecting a spark of the glory even in the most meager belief. The liturgy is a discipline; it leads us out into the light; it is work we are given to do under all conditions.

In the disciplines of Advent, as in life, the work precedes the glory. Scripture warns us not to be asleep on that day when the bridegroom comes, but to practice watching and waiting. These are to be our main occupations as we work for the kingdom. Prayer itself, in this time or any time, is a watchful expectancy for what God will do through the progression of days. We acknowledge that *we have not yet seen* the fullness of the light, all that God will do on our behalf. But from the little or much that we have seen and participated in already, God's acts are worth waiting for.

To kindle a light also indicates a desire to stay awake. We have to be able to view the path just ahead of our feet

in order to take it knowingly and certainly, even as darkness forms a kind of corridor around us. We are told that
the Lord is revealed to those who are awake, not to the
sleepers: to those who have lamps lit in expectation.

I am grateful for the sunlight today—what we have of
it—and for the guests who will come tonight and share our
table, to take what we have to offer of cheer and conversation around the fire.

It is good to be about the tasks of the day, whether we
work in much or little actual light. Soon we will be at the
point of increase as the days begin to get longer again—
gradually, imperceptibly at first.

I am reminded of the intriguing lines of Emily Dickinson's poem of the necessity of indirection, the kindness
inherent in a growing *process* that leads to dazzling realization of truth:

> As lightning to the Children eased
> With explanation kind
> The Truth must dazzle gradually
> Or every man be blind—

The Intermingling

Thou hast united, O Lord, thy divinity with our
humanity and our humanity with thy divinity.

*A*S I READ SCRIPTURE and other spiritual writings this Advent, I am being brought back again
and again to that central paradox of the Christian faith,
the incarnation itself. In the Syrian Liturgy of St. James
this doctrine is cast in the form of a prayer:

> Thou hast united, O Lord, thy divinity with our
> humanity and our humanity with thy divinity, thy
> life with our mortality and our mortality with thy
> life. Thou hast received what was ours and given
> unto us what was thine.

We cannot escape this startling fact. The intermingling
of the divine and human is part of God's plan, a promise
that was hinted at from the beginning in the initial planting of the tree of human life. God would deign to become
a branch from the stem of Jesse, Jesus Christ in the image
of the Father.

In the words of the Athanasian Creed, this intermingling
is "not by conversion of the Godhead into flesh; but by

taking of the Manhood into God." Yet there are hints of this exchange between God and us as early as Eden, in the lines in which the Lord tells the serpent, the usurper and tempter, "I will put enmity between you and the woman, and between your offspring and hers; he will strike your head, and you will strike his heel" (Gen. 3:15).

Enigmatic words, but they seem to indicate that God would join up with the human generations and actually work through flesh to bring about victory over the sons of deceit. This veiled prophecy forms an underlying basis for all other signs and hints of God's future reign. Though it would cost the death of God on a cross, this sacrifice would be a "bruise" of the body to bring about victory over evil. The slow path to God's coming in glory into our midst, which we anticipate in Advent, was to be written through time in the lives of the generations to follow this prediction.

An intermingling of the Godhead with humanity is that "scandal of particularity" that is so offensive and difficult to bear—a stumbling block to us as we face our own natures and own up to our unworthiness. But it is precisely to us, in our human condition, that the glory is so appealing. In our weakness and poverty we are not apt to think we had anything to do with manufacturing it ourselves. It is in the contrast of our sinfulness with God's grace that the miracle of the intermingling occurs, and we humbly agree to the redemption of our own flesh, by God's power alone.

The thought of such an intermingling requires some getting used to, and God gave ample opportunities for the patriarchs to see what this thread of redemption was to entail. God becoming flesh was surely foreshadowed in early appearances of Melchizedek, "king of Salem" and "priest of God Most High," to Abram. And instances of God's real presence as the "Angel of the Lord" can be found in the stories of the fourth "man" in the fiery furnace of Nebuchadnezzar and of Jacob's wrestling with the angel.

Though we try to separate the world of the flesh from the spirit, the overlapping and intermingling of the two thwart our own inclinations at every turn. It is in our own very human lives that God comes, redeeming these lives in the most physical of ways—teaching us through the span of actual days what it means to be God's, how our lives are "hid with Christ in God" for the duration. The pattern of Jesus' life and death is stamped upon us, and we grow to discover that mark indelible.

> Without any doubt, the mystery of our religion is great:
> > He was revealed in flesh,
> > > vindicated in spirit,
> > > > seen by angels,
> > > proclaimed among Gentiles,
> > > > believed in throughout the world,
> > > > > taken up in glory. (1 Tim. 3:16)

The formula here will hold for us as well. We are part of the paradox of the holiness of flesh as a vehicle of redemption. Our lives are a constant reminder that the Lord did desire such intimacy with humankind, and that our fate was bound up with God from the beginning.

At this time of the year it is natural to reflect on the incarnation, and to expect some overlapping of time and eternity in our thoughts. At this beginning of the church year we embark on the tracing of the mystery of the birth, life, and death of our Lord in God's time and in our history.

We acknowledge that the process of intermingling is sustained not only by the will of God, but by our participation. The power of human consent to God's plan has always mattered, from the "yes" of Abraham to follow God's call to a land he knew not—to move family and possessions, all the outward signs of his life, and go in faith. From Abraham to Mary, to the glorious consent of a young woman to bear a child into the world, we recognize a long line of faithful ones who have said "yes" to God and brought to fulfillment the centuries' sweep of prophecy and hope.

Always their consent was bought with a price—work, sweat, pain, risk of life—and surely they all faced darkness and uncertainty. We may sometimes forget that faith was always required of them, too, and that the outcome of their stories was not written in holy books before it occurred. All hung in a balance of human consent to the divine will—the plan for the intermingling entails those risks, and places such stock in flesh.

Who would dare to say "no" if we really knew a manifestation to be God, intruding in bodily form at the flap of the tent or commanding us in angel voices? It seems that the element of doubt would indeed excuse us, saying "I need more evidence," or asking, "Why me?" or pleading, "Not just yet, please ask again."

But the moment passes. The Lord is patient and long-suffering with the creation, but will not strive with us forever. Yet sometimes we have insurmountable doubts. So we wait for God to act in a way we can recognize and respond to, and sometimes we feel like Elijah on Mt. Carmel waiting for rain. He sent his servant six times to look toward the sea, only to be told, "There is nothing." But on the seventh time, the answer came, "Look, a little cloud no bigger than a person's hand is rising out of the sea" (1 Kgs. 18:43–44).

Clouds and burning bushes and voices and fire and smoke; waters of death to the enemy and of life to the thirsty; a prophet in the wilderness proclaiming the way of the Lord by self-denial and asceticism—all are signs and wonders that converge in the birth of a child called Emmanuel. God's work in all these signs employs the physical; God does not disdain to use earthly life in all its roughness—even a meager stable in a foreign city.

It is hard, constant work, to affirm the redemption of the body, to accept the intermingling. I wonder whether we err more often on the side of denying the incarnation than of taking divinity too lightly. In the conservative Protestant tradition in which I was brought up, Christ's divinity was held in such respect that we had to tread lightly with regard to any reference to his humanity (other than in specific biblical phrases that were undeniable). We were fearful of any reference to his humanity that might suggest that his nature was "common," or bring him down to our level. But God *did* bring him down—to us. Without the intermingling of the divine and human in him, and his stake in our humanity, there is no salvation. When I balk even now at the thought of Jesus as a human being, I am rescued again by the logic of Christian belief that, in Athanasius's words, "only that which is assumed is healed."

His assuming flesh—the whole human condition—may seem less formidable to us than his taking on the particular pains and ills, physical and psychological, that we see in ourselves and in other people.

Today as I was driving around in the city running a few

errands, I felt blindsided by the irritations and toils of daily physical existence, even under enviable conditions by the world's standards. Life is hard, especially in winter in the city: people waiting in the cold for their buses, or trudging through grimy snowbanks; children getting out of schools on dismal afternoons, crossing snow-filled asphalt playgrounds that emphasize the starkness of city living. Childhood isn't really as carefree and happy as it's made out to be—at least it wasn't for me, and today the children didn't look all that happy. In the cold and strain of difficult lives, how does love get a chance to break through?

How can Christians make the intermingling a reality to a world mired in hardship? How can a handful of worshipers in a particular parish church add any warmth to the world's cold, despite the powerful words and actions that go on inside its walls?

We proclaim, as a flicker of light against the bleakness, that Christ is indeed Lord of all life, and that in him— in his birth, life, death, and resurrection—human life is meant to be taken up out of itself and transformed into something glorious. The taking of human flesh into God is Christ's work, but it is also ours. We allow his taking of our human territory in small ways, acting in compassion and healing in his name, proclaiming the intermingling and its implications for all of creation.

In this season of Christ's birth we agree to exchange, to participation in the mystery of God-in-flesh. We do this best within the constraints of our own time and place, amid the limits of our bodies and what they can perform. Thus we grow to image forth the incarnation in small ways and bear witness with John that "the Word became flesh and lived among us . . . full of grace and truth."

Cradle and Cross

This little Babe so few days old,
Is come to rifle Satan's fold.

I T IS THE END of the first week in Advent. In this
journal, I had expected to write of softness and cradles
and sweet music and angels. Instead the Scripture passages, especially the prophets, have bombarded me with
images of suffering, judgment, warning, and persecution.
The verses I read in Isaiah 4 today have at least a hint of
hope in them, the expectation that all of creation will be
restored:

> On that day the branch of the LORD shall be
> beautiful and glorious, and the fruit of the land
> shall be the pride and glory of the survivors of
> Israel. (v. 2)

Hope of survival, longing for a day of peace, sustains us in
this season through the harsh predictions of what we may
yet have to live through, before the tree reaches its fullness
in glory.

We need these glints of God's promise of fruition and
deliverance when it seems, as it may in any age, impos-

sible that God should actually come to live among us. Yet
we cannot be disillusioned about the cost of peace. In
Luke 21 I read that the Temple will be destroyed, false
prophets will come, wars, earthquakes, persecutions, trials.
Yet God promises through all this to stand with us: "For
I will give you words and a wisdom that none of your op-
ponents will be able to withstand or contradict" (v. 15).

This, too, is Advent. It tells us of battles in which we
will join with Christ in the work that is to be done to bring
about the kingdom of God. For us it is too easy to think
only of the scenario of the cradle, a touching scene of beauty
and vulnerability. Some of the Advent carols I am listening
to hit at the heart of the paradox of softness and strength.
They offer, in poetic contrast, the scene of the infant in the
cradle alongside the harsh wood of the cross.

> *Sing lullaby!* Hush, do not wake the Infant King.
> Soon comes the cross, the nails, the piercing.
> Then in the grave at last reposing: *Sing lullaby!*

The nativity is not a complete scene without this element—
the cradle overshadowed by the cross—a reminder of the
whole scope of Christ's story. We must acknowledge sad-
ness mingled with the joy of birth, prepare for a note of
mourning embodied in the myrrh presented to a young
king.

The pinks and lavenders, the soft lights of children's
pageants, the velvets of a crèche under a tree—they seem
beautiful and tranquil in our recollections of Christmases
past, the capturing of a moment of exquisite joy. But they
stop short. Even in Christ's day his people Israel suffered
under bondage and persecution.

Today all of the words in Scripture of wars and con-
querings, famine and distress, always apply to some aspect
of the world's political and economic situation. We must
take heed to the word of threat and of promise. Christ is
always coming to us in the midst of distress; loving and
accepting, he is drawing us to himself. Yet he sits also in
judgment of the peoples, to do righteousness and bring
peace. In the meantime we sing: *"Hush, lullaby!"*

We do not celebrate the sleep of dreamers, which blocks
out reality. Rather we try to rest in the moment, as it is
given. Why strain? Worship him in the manger. "Come,
let us adore him." The hour of accounting for our salvation
will come soon enough. Do not grow weary looking for it;
be as wary as serpents and as harmless as doves.

In Robert Southwell's carol "This Little Babe" we find
another startling image of pain and glory, rest and striving:

> This little Babe so few days old,
> Is come to rifle Satan's fold;
> All hell doth at his presence quake,
> Though he himself for cold do shake.

The soft frailty of the baby is compared to a warrior
going into battle. In Southwell's carol the infant is God's
champion, carrying on the fight in the world against sin
and the devil. Christ's strength is made perfect in the
weakness of his infancy.

> For in this weak unarmèd wise
> The gates of hell he will surprise.
> With tears he fights and wins the field,
> His naked breast stands for a shield;

His battering shot are babish cries,
His arrows looks of weeping eyes,
His martial ensigns Cold and Need,
And feeble Flesh his warrior's steed.

However strange and inappropriate this imagery may seem to us in describing the manger scene, the poem attempts to fuse two realities and to warn the soul that more is at stake here than mere sweet lullabies at birth.

This little Babe will be thy guard.
If thou wilt foil thy foes with joy,
Then flit not from his heavenly Boy.

The verse does serve to remind us of the painful truth: that strain and toil come before the soft pleasures of a child new-born—suffering before victory. There is more to life than what is seen; the battle goes on behind the scenes.

Last night we went to an early Christmas service in my parents' Baptist church, where the season of Advent is not observed. I had not been in this church for ten years, and I was immediately struck by the lack of any religious symbol or decoration. The sanctuary was completely stark except for the Christian flag and the American flag, both flanking the pulpit. Was this early lack of visual images one reason that, as a child, I hungered for symbols of my faith in art, in poetry, in the richness of medieval splendor—for anything at all with gold leaf (I was very undiscriminating at first!), for carols of Mary and the Babe? Later I was intrigued by the implications of our redemption in the Christmas scenario until at one point I even played my Advent and Christmas tapes all year round as a comfort but also a kind of prayer.

Today I have another point of view. Reacting less to the past, more settled in an adult expression of my faith, I still savor the sounds and sights of the Advent season. My interest still lies in an earlier time, when the Christian year was incorporated into people's thinking in the general culture. Although life was harsh, the image of the Babe and the promise in that story could keep hearts from total despair over material deprivation.

We possess so much more nowadays—but do we possess as much spiritually? Medieval and Renaissance carols are so full of misery, understood corporately, as our condition and lot. They portray redemption through the poor child who appears weak and helpless, but is God's chosen one, launched into the world to rout evil and conquer in the end. His tender softness precedes pain, a pain that in turn precedes glory and victory. It is a cycle, but one rooted in our history, with a glorious, promised culmination for which we still wait.

Another of Southwell's carols, "In Freezing Winter Night," bids us:

Behold a silly tender babe,
In freezing winter night,
In homely manger trembling lies;
Alas, a piteous sight!

The inns are full; he is forced to a "pilgrim bed"—the symbol of our own sojourn. But he is a babe we can identify with in his humanity and need, and we share with him in the expectation of glory. We are part of his story; we claim his history and join in his suffering as our own. His cradle is our beginning point too; we are babes in our helplessness. In his weakness, paradoxically, is our strength, our deliverance.

As Christians we cannot see the cradle without perceiving the cross suspended over it—the hard wood of both, united in purpose. We contemplate in Advent the circumstances of the stable, harsh and bare, the prospect of poverty and rejection that was to be Jesus' lot on earth. Perhaps total barrenness and lack of ornament in worship can also serve to draw us to him. Absence of visible glory reminds us that someday the inner light will shine out and be revealed. Ornamentation, or lack of it, is a matter of style, which is as important in worship as it is in love. Equally by the denial of images or the affirmation of them as signposts, by the words of a carol or a melody alone, we may be drawn to that One in the manger, the King to come.

Advent Two

Merciful God, who sent your messengers the prophets to preach repentance and prepare the way for our salvation: Give us grace to heed their warnings and forsake our sins, that we may greet with joy the coming of Jesus Christ our Redeemer; who lives and reigns with you and the Holy Spirit, one God, now and for ever.

Repent! Praise!

Prepare the way of the Lord,
make his paths straight.

TODAY IN HIS SERMON, my husband startled me by illustrating Advent—a time of waiting and preparing for the Lord—as a couple anticipating and making ready for the birth of a child. He spoke of the long months of hoping, watching for any promise of new life; the stirrings, the changes, the prayers for a safe delivery. Finally, there is the joy of birth—a parallel to the time when Jesus is born anew in our hearts at Christmas.

Of course, such analogies are very much on our minds. In fact, there was a birth in the parish yesterday of a boy named Christopher—Christ-bearer—whose mother happened to be named Mary. We could not help but experience some identification with their joy as we anticipate the birth of our own child.

Thus in Advent the tension between joy-in-waiting and joy-set-loose continues to confront us. We may be in a time of repentance, discipline, examination, even self-denial to some extent. Yet reasons to praise keep breaking through! We are reminded in Psalm 149 that the Lord takes pleasure in us, and that it is good to give thanks as our numbers here grow.

How are we to praise in Advent? Today all three of the designated Psalms begin with "Praise the Lord!" Sunday is always a reminder of resurrection joy, even in this season—a day when we come together to lift our hearts and voices to the Lord. We are thankful for God's mercy to us to this point in our lives, as we travel the weeks toward Christmastide.

But how are we to keep in tension the necessary work of repentance while continuing to praise? John the Baptist, an important figure we focus upon in Advent, helps us to see how the two must go together in our understanding of new life. He proclaimed the coming of the Lord during the Roman occupation of Palestine, a time when it was very hard to believe. He preached repentance to the hard of heart. Yet his whole ministry also embodied praise; all his words and actions pointed to the worthiness of Christ.

There had always been prophets, but this man was different. John the Baptist came with a fresh and visible sign, old in origin but new in application, and he cleansed with water those who desired a new beginning, a baptism, a clean slate before God. John witnessed to Jesus by his ascetic life and single-mindedness—some would say mania—for one purpose. He came to make the way straight, to prepare hearts for Messiah.

John broke through the rigorism and ignorance of God that existed even among keepers of the Law. And in the new guise of denial and hardship this new prophet challenged his hearers to take the old prophets seriously. He proclaimed that the Word of the Lord was alive and active, cutting deeply into their own time and place with specific injunctions. *Repent! Praise!* Laziness and indifference would not suffice. Here was a claim to messiahship to be reckoned with: One was coming to set things straight with God. Great changes were imminent whether the people were ready or not.

John the Baptist represents the call to radical preparation of one's whole life for the coming of the kingdom. His is an extreme message, and his own story ends in an early death. Yet while he lived, he praised the Lord with his whole being, his habits, his reputation, his life—for all it was worth. He brought the messages of the Old Testament prophets, especially of Isaiah, into focus, and validated the hope expressed so long ago. A way, a path to God, would be prepared. "A voice cries out, 'In the wilderness prepare the way of the LORD, make straight in the desert a highway for our God'" (Isa. 40:3).

The call to repentance must always precede praise. Acknowledging sin clears the way for the truth of God's deliverance, for the Messiah to come into his own. And praise naturally follows the revelation of truth. John was the last forerunner of the Lord, a close earthly relation of Jesus. He had even leaped in his mother Elizabeth's womb at the announcement that Christ would be born into the world, a foreshadowing of his prophetic mission to praise and acknowledge Messiah with his whole being.

The connection between repentance and praise that the Baptist exemplifies is a fitting one in Advent, helping us to balance our spirits between joy-in-waiting and joy-set-loose.

This afternoon we attended an ecumenical Advent service, a musical festival of many voices. Unfortunately, the church it was held in had already been decorated for Christmas. It is hard to keep our Episcopalian spirit of Advent in such a setting, with different denominations' expectations and traditions all melded into a community affair. Yet our choice to be with other Christians in a place of worship, to do the self-examination and praising of this season as we can, counts for something. A desire for alertness, awareness, and a sincere response to God keep us actively worshiping.

One way we are able to be consistent in our own services is to rely on the Book of Common Prayer for praise that is fitting to the time—along with confession, which is always appropriate to our condition. When our mouths are taught to follow these thought-out and time-tested forms, in sequence, the repetition and our consistency can serve to bring our hearts along. Proclaiming *Lord, I believe, help my unbelief,* is an honest prayer and underlies our best attempts at balancing confession and praise.

It is a subtle task to keep praising in a season such as Advent. Sometimes it seems too much of an effort to keep the paradoxes alive—repentance and joy, expectation and praise. I wonder, do my weak strains of praise, in my circumstances, with my particular understanding of the season, make any difference in the vast throng? Yet I believe the discipline of being present with the broader church and contributing in some way is preferable to overexamining every nuance, being overscrupulous about keeping Advent.

We always have a choice of what to focus on—at any time there are twenty things going wrong, fifty to be unhappy about. But praise refocuses us on God's work in our midst in this and any season. It teaches us to look for evidence of Christ's coming to us, his redemption being prepared for us, even at this moment. We meet with other Christians in a place designed to contain praise. We come to hear again the story of God's grace in which repentance is ongoing, an inner chord echoing in our hearts. As long as we are in God's presence and each other's company, we can live in this time of waiting and yet celebrating.

John's message is part of our own story. In Advent we all take the parts of those who proclaim the coming of Christ—for in our calendar he has not yet come. We can participate in the process of revealing the truth of his coming through Scripture, as the drama gradually unfolds in prayer and prophecy and spectacular event.

While Episcopal churches consider Christmas carols out of place during Advent, no matter where you go in this season—including the service we went to this afternoon—you are likely to hear "Silent Night" and "Hark, the Herald Angels Sing," as though to get a jump on the festival of Christmas. Some of the earlier medieval and Renaissance carols that include both the cross and the tomb come closer to the spirit of Advent because they acknowledge the fullness of revelation, of which Advent is only the beginning. They hint at the whole scope of the Christmas story that starts again in this season.

In Advent we talk of preparing, of waiting, and therefore it would be almost impossible to avoid mentioning *what* it is we are waiting for, and *why*. Yet our emphasis on repentance, intermingled with praise, can sometimes give our songs a minor key. In these days we need to consider our own condition, and dare to think, "What if he had not come?" Our redemption hangs in the balance, and "all lies in a passion of patience" (Charles Williams's fine phrase) as we wait.

We pray that he will come to our hearts, as he did in the lives of those faithful believers: Mary, John, Anna, Simeon,

Elizabeth. Acknowledgment of our own unworthiness, yet acceptance of the gift—two distinct actions—are as inseparable in us as they were in those saints. Our belief, like their hope, is part of the ongoing story of redemption. We are brought into line with the whole event through repentance and praise.

Glimpses of Glory

Merciful God, who sent your messengers the prophets to
preach repentance and prepare the way for our salvation:
Give us grace to heed their warnings and forsake our
sins.

*T*HE COLLECT FOR the second week in Advent reminds us that it is a time to listen hard to the prophets' words that trace the coming steps of our Redeemer
and lighten our way.

In Isaiah 2 today I read that "the mountain of the LORD's
house shall be established," that our God will reign in Zion
and "judge between the nations" (vv. 2, 4)—a pronounce-
ment for the future of Judah and Jerusalem at the time,
with echoes of a final triumphant reign yet to come. This
glimpse of coming glory appears first in the reading; next
Isaiah tells us that people's lives could not sustain such
glory as yet, because they are materialists in a land filled
with idols, who would be more likely to hide before the
terror of the Lord than to enter into peace.

Something must happen in the meantime, say the prophets, before redemption is fulfilled. The more I read the Old
Testament prophets, the clearer it seems that all relay the
same message: We have erred, gone our own way, but One

will come to make it right. All creation longs for that day when God alone will be exalted (v. 11).

Today I feel a need for some glimpse of this coming event, a flash of the promised glory. With snow showers and only intermittent sunshine, it is hard to envision the light prevailing. I want to immerse myself in thoughts of Advent, but I keep encountering the cost as well as the rewards of Jesus' coming. I believe in the images of hope offered us by the prophets; but through what, I wonder, will the world—including those of us alive today—have to live before we see that day?

In our parish this season, we are seeing some hopeful signs of the coming kingdom. Relationships are being healed, new people are volunteering for needed tasks—all steps toward unity of purpose and spirit. The church is for us a visible sign of God's presence here and now, in this place. In the cooperative effort to maintain and support a ministry, there are encouragements as well as setbacks.

In this mix of "signs," Advent is like every other season. But Advent speaks to us in this place of the urgency of commitment, of joining up with the procession that will meet the Bridegroom when he comes. In concrete ways, these faithful people have braved the grayness winter after winter, continuing in worship and expectation. We are all an encouragement to each other that each day, each year has purpose as we grow in preparation to hail the dawn of God's coming into our lives.

Through our worship, our liturgy, we affirm again and again that the prophets spoke in truth, that their message lives—even as we struggle to believe, to pronounce again the goodness of creation. We continue to have faith and affirm that what God set in motion was worth it; that daily life with its toil and pain is compensated for by the joy that is set before us.

I cannot imagine the fullness of Christ's coming in glory. My tastes are not yet rich enough, nor my eyes sharp enough. But I can readily acknowledge the joys that are mine now, in a life approaching middle maturity: a settled, inner peace, married love, a contentment in my work. The intricate beauty of these, God's gifts, would have been unfathomable to me in earlier days. As my own journey continues, I cannot help but feel that it is to be part of the fabric of glory for which we look, that God's mending of brokenness and healing of hearts in particular lives is a way of building the kingdom and preparing for its glory.

All I can assume is that whatever joys await us in the coming Day of the Lord are far—and farther—beyond us than our adult fulfillments loomed beyond our childhoods. Our own passages in time are, I am convinced, a way of increasing our capacity for glory.

I believe it will be worth it to be human in that moment, though some of us have traveled the long road around, through painful failures, stumblings, setbacks. We are assured in Romans that "the sufferings of this present time are not worth comparing with the glory about to be revealed to us" (8:18). Somehow, it seems to be saying, we are destined to be written into the script in order to share in the glory.

It takes faith in any age to believe in the goodness of the Lord and in future healing of this broken world. The newspaper headlines make us wish that today Christ would come to judge between the nations and decide for the people—we seem incapable of deciding rightly for ourselves. We long for the peaceful sign of plowshares rather than swords, for transformation and corporate restoration on a grander scale than we seem to be allowed to see.

We cannot measure how much work must and will be done before the path to justice becomes clear and Jesus reigns over the earthly order. Our own work along that path of repentance and peace seems plodding, ineffectual much of the time. Yet we choose to believe that history is going somewhere, and that it will lead toward that final consummation.

I am aware that each day of work matters, just as what I choose now to do with my body each day matters to someone besides myself. I want to continue in prayer, worship, praise for another day, thanksgiving for food and rest, shelter and loved ones. I want to be able to tell my child that this continuing in life matters, that we press on even through patches of haziness when we temporarily lose sight of the glory. We can reimmerse ourselves in God's Word, in communion with other believers, in service, to keep going until the cloud passes and our sight improves.

I am thankful for a tradition in which I can raise my child to have familiarity with the images of glory that shine through Scripture and the liturgy, that keep us looking up. Hopes such as these surely have their childlike counterparts to keep young hearts believing in goodness: the toys on Christmas morning, a park in the fall, a new dress, a loving pet—all these gifts tease and mellow us to prepare us for the real thing.

I struggle myself, day by day, as broken things hamper my vision. Yesterday I bent the key in the back door lock and it broke off in the cold. Late this afternoon I broke the coffee canister. These are small frustrations that don't amount to much, but losses can make it even harder to have faith that all things are being mended and brought together, that Christ will reign over a completed, unbroken kingdom.

A Eucharist will take place tonight at the church. It is a healing service for all who desire the oil of anointing, the laying on of hands for their own healing and that of others through intercessory prayer. It reminds me of the opportunity for proclaiming Christ that my husband has been given in his office of priest. He is privileged to invoke the powerful name of Jesus, each time, at the laying on of hands, affirming for us in our weak faith (and his own, at times) that "there is no other name in heaven or earth under which our health and salvation reside, but the one name Jesus Christ the Lord."

The house of the Lord will be established, and its beginnings are here, today.

Lord, give us grace to believe the word of your prophets.

Icons of the Kingdom

Be at peace among yourselves . . . admonish the idlers,
encourage the faint hearted, help the weak, be patient
with all of them.

I WAS A BIT LATE arriving at the Episcopal Church
Women's meeting this afternoon, and when I entered
the parish hall, the room had already been darkened for a
slide show on icons that was to be given by a guest speaker,
a professor from a nearby college.

Displayed on the screen was an icon depicting Christ's
birth at Bethlehem, as an introduction to the topic of Eastern Orthodox art. This one scene captured in essence for
me the Orthodox sensibility about incarnation; it por-
trayed earthiness and glory residing comfortably side by
side. A triptych of the birth story, it showed simultaneously Christ lying in the manger, Christ being bathed by a
maid, and his mother, Mary, reclining after childbirth—all
human poses and actions that would occur at a real birth. I
was deeply touched by this honesty, amid the beauty of the
art style, and thought of all the many pretty nativity scenes
that show Mary fully recovered after childbirth, kneeling
before her infant son—a worthy response, but hardly a com-

fortable or even possible position after real labor and delivery, I would think!

I have always been intrigued by icons, and find just this sort of human detail so appealing because, rather than separating us from the historical event, it offers us a bridge of understanding. The human element helps us imagine what it might have been like and allows us to bring our own weaknesses and limitations along in our response to the newborn king. In such depictions, our humanity is "assumed" as Christ assumed it, or took it on; it is not relegated to the unholy, but brought into the beauty of God's plan without apology.

We wanted to have this presentation in Advent, for the incarnation underlies all that is to follow. But the speaker made it clear also that the feast of Christmas in Orthodox worship and art is overshadowed by the number and prominence of icons found on the resurrection. In contrast, icons of the crucifixion are displayed not in the sanctuary but near places of burial, as reminders of death and the hope of eternal life. The church lives in the light of resurrection, the flowering of the doctrine of the incarnation. And thus God's house on earth is filled with icons that celebrate the glory of our heavenly habitation, toward which we process: the New Jerusalem.

All this is a reminder to me that the church is a picture of what God's kingdom is to be, a sign of its presence in the world among and in God's people. The in-Godding begins here—as taught in the Orthodox doctrine of divinization, the gradual taking on of Christ's nature through his dwelling in us and we in him. Peter writes: "His divine power has given us everything needed for life and godliness, through the knowledge of him who called us by his own glory ... that ... you may escape from the corruption that is in the world because of lust, and may become participants of the divine nature" (2 Pet. 1:3–4).

The beauty and other-worldliness of the icons (in contrast to their sometimes earthy detail) is a reminder that it is possible to live in the world but not be of it. We can be clear about our destination even as we go about our daily work, and be conscious of reflecting and affirming the resurrection in our own bodies while we live.

Orthodox icons and worship are inseparable. The joy of life is mirrored in both. I once knew an Orthodox priest who, when asked by someone why his people kissed icons, replied, "Because it's fun." In all reverence, his human joy in the visual representations of his beliefs naturally overflowed into worship.

Many of the icons shown today were of the face of Christ, and the speaker pointed out that the Orthodox believe that graven images were forbidden by God to Israel *before* Christ came to earth and gave us a picture of himself in human form. His incarnation, actual birth in flesh, and revelation of himself as of the very nature of God, changed things forever. As Christ represents the "scandal of particularity" in his person, so religious belief can now incorporate the risk of depicting God in flesh, and thus point unbelievers to the truth and strengthen the faith of those who already believe.

I had always heard that icons represented "windows into heaven," glimpses of the glory of the life to come, hinted at in gold leaf and vivid colors suggesting fullness of life. But our speaker countered this view by pointing out that we don't really need windows so much as eyes that are opened up to see what is around us here, in this life. For in Orthodox thought heaven is not so much another place that needs to be peered into, but rather the quality of life in Christ that begins here through the power of his resurrection.

In this view, eternal life includes the day-to-day getting there, the faithful journey of the saints as they are permitted glimpses of glory that punctuate everyday life, especially as they are revealed to us in corporate worship. No wonder Orthodox services tend to be so long—with seemingly endless choir responses and many opportunities to grasp the beauty and joy of resurrection, especially as it is celebrated in the season of Easter.

I was glad that the first icon we saw was one of Jesus' birth, because nativity is clearly brought up into the fullness of inclusion with the themes of incarnation and resurrection that so dominate the Orthodox faith. I am feeling again the fullness of expectation of this time of year, with the next stops on the Christian calendar looming. The rhythms are already set in motion by the acknowledgment of Advent and the invitation to step into this flow of days and participate in it fully.

The Orthodox encourage this participation in many tactile ways: They kiss icons, paint murals in beautiful colors, light candles, and have almost ethereal music. Children are welcomed to their celebration of the heavenly meal of thanksgiving—the Eucharist. One tradition is that all partake of both wine and host administered together in a spoon. While some outside the tradition may ask whether children can really know what they are doing in taking communion, the Orthodox ask, "Does anyone really know?"

It always remains a mystery, as impenetrable by intellect

alone at any age. But of this they are sure: It is best entered into with confidence that God's gifts are offered for all of us, and we cannot receive them as mere bystanders. As the Orthodox point out, faith is not primarily a rational thing. Mere knowledge of facts or even of doctrines is not what true religion is about. Belief itself can hardly be systematic; it is, rather, a quality of life and practice.

I am glad that in the Anglican tradition theology is not over-systematized. Its western expression may be more structured and rational than that of the Orthodox, but it also tends to the freer forms of theological reflection, based on historical, scriptural, and literary examples of faith. We are able to include our own experience. We often draft statements and draw conclusions, but do not exclude mystery, awe, and reverence. So the spiritual sensibility of Anglicanism, like the style of the Orthodox, is best expressed in its worship.

One of the things that most attracts me to this tradition of spirituality is the way the Orthodox use language to describe the progress of the soul, both here on earth and on its way to heaven. Language itself can be a vehicle of truth, as are the icons, but we can never expect to exhaust its possibilities or use it to define all that our belief entails.

Language of the soul does its best work when it does not attempt to be rationally explicit, but rather conveys truth with the accuracy of poetry—which on its own terms can be as revealing as rational discourse. The Orthodox, for example, speak of the dying as those who "fall asleep in the Lord," and they trust that those souls will "find rest and peace in the kingdom which God has for them until the day when God comes at the end of all things." What more can any of us really say about the mystery inherent in the state of the dead? We can speculate on the scriptural language—but we can't actually add much to it. However, we can prepare for our own death, which is one intent of worship and of continuing to practice our faith.

Scripture, of course, gives us guidelines for how to live that faith while we are on the way. For instance, in our reading today I find Paul calling the Thessalonians to a way of living that surely partakes of heaven here: "Be at peace among yourselves . . . admonish the idlers, encourage the faint hearted, help the weak, be patient with all of them. See that none of you repays evil for evil. . . . Rejoice always, pray without ceasing, give thanks in all circumstances; for this is the will of God in Christ Jesus for you. Do not quench the Spirit. . . . Hold fast to what is good; abstain from every form of evil" (1 Thess. 5:13–22). Surely living by these standards is part of the in-othering here on earth, and also a way of becoming icons of the truth of heaven to one another.

I believe the icons call us to consider what we are meant to be to each other—"little Christs," tangible evidence of the truth of the incarnation. Every day we encounter unique (though flawed) examples of God's handiwork in others. Just as icons are human art, we in our bodies are manifestations of the goodness of creation and the beauty of God's work.

I keep thinking of that first icon I saw of Mary and Joseph, no doubt because of its relevance to me as I look forward to giving birth. As Christ is part of that icon's scene, he is also part of my scenario. He is my hope and my help, reminding me that every opportunity to reveal his power in the world has a physical side, a human task. His dual nature, his humanity and divinity, interact with me at every point in my life, because I am called to share in his life.

The in-Godding begins here. All I can do, which is exactly what I am called to do, is offer up the circumstances of my life, allowing myself to be an icon of sorts. In embodying Christ my life can be redeemed for some purpose, made useful for the kingdom.

The Pain of Delay

Wait for the Lord*;*
be strong, and let your heart take courage;
wait for the Lord*!*

WRITING HAS SO MANY frustrations. Yesterday a feature article I had been assigned to write for a publication came back to me after I had thought I was through with it. The editor asked for some revision, which required several hours of writing last evening and rereading this morning. Then I had to retype it, photocopy it at the library, and frantically rush to the post office in hopes of getting it delivered by the next business day's mail. I am never sure if things will arrive on time and, as an editor myself, I know what a day or two can cost in efficiency down the line in producing a book or magazine.

Writing is a very independent sort of work, and it takes some confidence to say things boldly that are intended for print and then let them go into someone else's hands. There they can be misplaced, misunderstood, garbled, poorly edited—or gracefully trimmed and enhanced for publication so that you look better than you deserve. There is a painful gap, a delay between your thinking the piece through, the actual writing, and a tangible sign of what the outcome of your labor will be. Sometimes the articles and projects that you feel best about don't even sell, and, as they never see the light of day, it is as though you never created them. At best, you may profit and grow from learning to live with delay and disappointment! Yet sometimes, years later, you are actually relieved that someone spared you the embarrassment of placing your premature intellectual gropings in print.

The pain of delay is always present in any process that depends on a network. Writers can wait months, even years, before they see any fruit of their hard work. In the meantime, the writer will have grown and may have even forgotten what drove her to write as she did. As one writer I know confesses, when she gets galley proofs of her books to read over, it is like eating stewed tissue paper. As important as the words once seemed, often we can find not only the delay, but the fruition as well, painful or insipid.

Then why would anyone want to take up a career in writing? As I was told in journalism school, don't go into writing unless you can't do anything else. My professor was not referring to skill, but rather to the compulsion to put down in words and see in print one's own work, regardless of the pain and lack of rewards. Another test for writers is to consider, when you are writing, whether you feel an urge to be doing something else instead. If not, then you know that writing is what you are meant to be about.

I remember a story Madeleine L'Engle tells of receiving yet another rejection for her novel *A Wrinkle in Time*. Rather than giving up writing altogether, she found her mind naturally leading her to a new project—a book on failure. It was never written, as *Wrinkle* found both its publisher and audience and went on to win a Newbery Medal.

Yet the pain of delay, even to a writer already published, tends to throw one back to questioning the whole enterprise from the beginning. Was I really called to this? Will I ever find an audience?

I have read interviews with actors in which they admit, even after a successful film or theater run, that they always doubt they will ever work again. It seems in some professions that depend on performance (and writing is a kind of performance that is literally cast in ink), you are only as good as your present success, at least in your own mind.

Writing this journal is a quiet performance in the privacy of my world, as I fit it into the rest of my ordered life. I must also work on assignments that are already slated to fit into designated editorial space. Why work so hard at something unasked for? There is certainly risk in exposing yourself to the pain of delay, the possibility of rejection, by taking on a task of your own design. There is a hiddenness to my work on these pages, not so different from the interiority of a child being formed inside its mother. And the delivery of a book, though different, also launches you into a new situation.

I have found it best not to put all my hopes in one aspect of the writing I do, but to keep venturing into new markets with unsolicited material, sending out reworked pieces and trying revised forms, being open to new avenues of expression; this is necessary, if you really want to write.

The more you send "out there," of course, the more possibilities of pain, delay, and rejection—but also the more chances for acceptance. One outweighs the other. Rejections are easier to take in the context of hitting some markets right; you may forget about your precious work when it is legion—and sometimes acceptances come as pure gift. The work you sent out months earlier is not even on your mind when working on some new project.

I find the pain of delay is not alien to Advent thinking both in the areas of spirituality and practical work. Delay is not failure; it is waiting for the "fullness of time," in which things can be revealed as what they truly are. For the writer, delay can trigger a process that allows the sifting of the valuable from the shallow and self-indulgent in one's thinking. In time the writer can move from having to defend his point of view in anger or reaction, to a more gracious unfolding of ideas that will build up and edify. A humility can come, through maturity and hard knocks, and the ability to admit, not that *I've got it all right,* but that this is one way of viewing a problem or an idea, and I offer it as a facet of the truth. As a writer I may grow to welcome honest dialogue, disagreement, or amplification, and even having others point out my blind spots.

The pain of delay can also reveal what kernel of truth was there in the early stumblings to write and be heard. Through the process of active waiting, a writer can find the correct genre to be working in, can let other attempts drop away, gain courage to say things that may be controversial but bring clarity—and, ideally, greater love—to the task and to the audience as well.

The cost of delay has everything to do with the pain of having layers peeled from your ego and allowing rejections, disappointments, and struggles with impatience to build up the inner person. The outer is toughened, making you better able to take the shocks and hurts, and keep at it. Just as continuing to choose to perform marks an artist, I think that continuing to write, alone, is what marks a writer. In fact, the present tense *I write* is probably more accurate than to say *I am a writer.*

To the degree that the artist or writer is able to be honest in his or her work, it will be revealed whether or not there is real substance in it after all. Does the fullness of time reveal it as divisive, or does it expand our loves? Were we in it for ourselves all the time, or is there an element of ministry in our work, of openness to God's Spirit to use the gift, no more or less than any other, but clearly for good? Those are questions that can be answered only in time, through discipline, through transparency, through willingness to be accountable to our audience and to God.

So many of the Psalms I have read and lived by through the years encourage waiting through this pain of delay. We believe that God does not give gifts or desires so as to frustrate us for our lifetime, nor to deny us the incentive and encouragement to keep on. Psalm 27 encourages us:

> Wait for the LORD;
>> be strong, and let your heart take courage;
>> wait for the LORD! (v. 14)

This is a fine prayer for bridging the pain of delay, both in writing and in other times of waiting.

Dependence on others—editors, publishers, market analysts, and trends that can change overnight and make an editorial or an article obsolete—is part of the healthy accountability that forces writers to realize they must catch as catch can. When pieces are accepted, it does not always mean we're especially gifted, but merely that we have filled a current need that someone else perceives. Sometimes, we humbly admit, our words have merely filled an empty space.

On the other hand, the pain of rejection, of delay that seems endless, may not mean we lack talent or our work is inferior. There are dozens of reasons why a piece may not be accepted, including the mood of the first reader that morning. And when something does click, it is because a number of factors (many beyond our influence) all worked together to make it go; in other words, from our point of view, it is grace.

I was just reading the review of a book that a woman wrote about her famous parents, and someone asked her, "Who wants to read about someone else's family?" A good question, the author admitted; yet she countered that every story is about someone's relatives, real or imagined. Who wants to read someone else's thought processes, someone's private journal? Other people who have some of the same feelings, perhaps, or similar experiences that they strive to make sense of. Readers who feel reassured or challenged or touched by reminders of what we share in this life, who value different perspectives and others' perceptions of God in their particular circumstances.

It is a risk, nevertheless, to write and publish, to put it all out for display and judgment. The pain of delay sometimes leads to the pain of fulfillment, which can be a nightmare as well as a dream come true. It is all part of the cost of incarnation, of enfleshing what is mind and spirit in risky forms such as print, which can then be rejected. Why would anyone want to be a writer, anyway?

In the face of all this, for me, writing is another way of allowing Christ to be born in and through me, perhaps revealed to others in a slight glimpse through the dance of language. It is a chance at least to point to the truth, if not to persuade, and to offer someone else a reason to hope.

A Way to Live

*Take delight in the L*ORD*,*
and God will give you the desires of your heart.

*T*ODAY I AM FACING some decisions about my own
commitment within the parish. Super-woman expectations of ministers' wives have been ingrained in me from
the early years I spent in a small, struggling church. These
memories nag at me and tell me that my presence, active
participation, and volunteer labor are considered part of
the package to the people my husband pastors.

Yet a wife's role is never made explicit when a married
clergyman accepts a call. And today, the "extra worker" expectation is not always realistic, as so many wives work
outside the home, many of them in professional positions.
Yet I harbor doubts as to whether I'm doing enough, am
present as often as I could be, or am willing to take on
tasks that are boring or that I feel are completely unsuited
to my skills.

I am very committed to my professional work, though
I think few people understand that or even see my working as a factor in our situation. My trade is quiet and un-
obtrusive. Parishioners don't necessarily read what I write;
some of it hasn't even come out in print yet. The circles

of my colleagues are far removed from this neighborhood and its particular concerns. In most ways, I feel my work is invisible to parishioners—and some people don't quite consider writing to be "work," anyway. I remember the cartoon in which one woman asks another, "Does your husband work now, or is he still writing?"

Being a writer is seen as comparable to being a painter or poet and waiting for that big "break" that never comes—a lazy person's excuse for not doing anything else in the meantime. People identify much more readily with other aspects of my life: home and husband, entertaining and personal interests. Working in service groups in the church especially helps to connect my life with those of other women. Right now I am a member of the Altar Guild and part of a book study group and a prayer cell. Yet beyond thoughts of my personal usefulness or my contribution, my main concern is over how long to continue my involvement for the sake of the other people. I am extremely cautious in what I take on, because once I've committed myself I hate to let anyone down; and I know that my continued visibility and sharing of the parish ministry is extremely important.

Also, I know I need group participation in my life in order to balance my own very solitary tendencies. When given a choice, I'm almost too happy to stay with my books and typewriter and have the opportunity to do independent research and writing. I need to be forced to join and involve myself in a group—it does not come naturally to me. Therefore the invisible expectations are in some ways a mercy, which works for good.

Now, however, I am aware that I'm working in a shortened time frame. Before long I won't be able to attend evening meetings or volunteer for service without having to find child care. And my continued health and stamina—as well as the health of the baby—are unknowns at this point. I want to pace myself through these months, complete the projects I've already agreed to, and not start too many new ones. But since we haven't told anyone here about the baby yet, some of my decisions appear not to have any foundation. I turned down an offer to help deliver Meals on Wheels, a refusal that I know was misunderstood. But it would break up my working day, and the time involved is more than I can handle now; I would have had to give it up in a few months anyway, with the prospect of a newborn in my life.

Whenever I'm frustrated and wondering if I'm thinking straight, or too self-centeredly, I turn to the Psalms. I find it most natural to pray with the meditative ones; like the Psalmist, I assume an I–Thou relationship with God. The poet's cries and needs so often reflect my own soul's search.

> Prove me, O LORD, and try me;
> > test my heart and mind.
> For your steadfast love is before my eyes,
> > and I walk in faithfulness to you. (Ps. 26:2–3)

Although I know my own failures and weaknesses intimately, my *desire* is to follow the way of righteousness reflected in this prayer. And I find the wisdom passages in Psalms (and in the bulk of the Book of Proverbs) further teach me a way to live. They give me perspective on whatever problem or decision I am up against—including my present doubts about parish service.

What I share with the writers is my belief in God's transcendence as well as immanence in the world, whether in mighty acts, so often described anthropomorphically in these texts (the work of God's hands and the breath of God's mouth) or in the assurance of the Lord's presence wherever I go (Ps. 139:8–10). In this Old Testament wisdom I find guidance that fits my own "inscape"—my inner workings. The scenery is familiar to me, and my soul responds to the consciousness in these lines. In lines such as these in Psalm 37, I find a way to approach my dilemma:

> Trust in the LORD, and do good;
>> so you will live in the land, and enjoy security.
> Take delight in the LORD,
>> and God will give you the desires of your heart.
> Commit your way to the LORD . . . (vv. 3–5)

I rely on the immediacy of this advice, the assurance of peace, and the encouragement that there is something one can do in the face of decisions. The outcome, finally, will not come apart from relationship—a trust in the One who has led me this far, in these particular paths. *There is a way to live.*

Wisdom, as expressed by the poet, conveys a confidence that we are not in the world alone, or operating on principles that we thought up ourselves yesterday. God set all things on earth in motion, and we have an underlying faith that the Lord will not forsake us, that in some sense order will prevail.

There is sophisticated thinking about reality here, a depth in the ancient lines that is still fresh in its simplicity of expression. Even without New Testament revelation we can discover in these words how to please God and live in the light. For the way of wisdom in these passages is intended to be passed on, so that the individual need not reinvent morality or good sense in each generation. In Israel, age and experience were acknowledged as worthy and as evidence of wisdom. The rabbis had something to teach from their own lives' search and contemplation in the areas of law and practice. Thus their followers, whether in formal schools of wisdom or the school of life, could be lifted up on the shoulders of their teachers' examined lives.

This view of wisdom expressed as an ideal in Scripture brings my own very real questions into clearer focus. As long as I truly desire what is pleasing to God and best for myself and others in these areas of service and use of time, the way will be made clear to me how to choose. Wisdom thinking does still work today—but not as a merely pragmatic method of self-help. It always includes the Lord, and requires our openness to God's will, through waiting, expectation, and sincere willingness to act in the opportune time.

For the people of Israel, it was reassuring to affirm that God was enthroned as king over all. Because of this rule, order was possible; actions had logical consequences in the world, with room for apparent paradoxes and uncertainties from our limited human perspective.

Nevertheless, God was sovereign and could also be expected to act, in God's own time—and in the people's earthly time. All the workings of society could be traced to that theocratic principle, so that the enthroning of Israel's earthly king was a visible sign of solidarity and order—much more concrete evidence than we have today. While ancient peoples had to battle to preserve national order over chaos, sometimes I think we are no farther along. Today the chaos we fight off is within our own hearts as well as in society.

The Psalms remind us that others have tread this human journey and fought these battles, have known this spiritual landscape. In some ways their pilgrimage is not so different from our own. It is a privilege to be able to read their recorded wisdom, unequaled in any later prayers. This lasting quality of biblical language is one way in which Scripture bears the mark of inspiration: its ability to uncover truth in the accuracy of poetry. I always feel I can't go far wrong in leaning toward its wisdom. And perhaps this too is what stirs me in the Psalms: I can imagine how my own life fits into such a view. The poet's language is descriptive, accurately evoking inner struggles such as those I am facing, with enough ambiguity for me to apply it to my particular situation.

One reason I have always loved English poetry is that it tends to *suggest* rather than to spell out, leaving room for one's own imagination to complete the particulars. There is some of that openness and universality in Hebrew poetry too, although we constantly encounter memorably concrete images as well. For instance, a phrase such as "All flesh is grass," although concrete, is also wide open and timeless. We can fill in that image in a million ways—envisioning days of experience, of aging, of flourishing for a time, of being mowed down. Until (if ever) the whole world becomes paved with Astroturf, we will all know what grass is and be able to relate to this image's particularity and broad applicability.

Part of the work of images is to uplift the soul, including

the imagination, and in the Psalms I find hope; I am able to affirm my connection with the whole repository of Old Testament wisdom. Immersing myself in these phrases and verses, I find the peace of understanding that *there is a way to go in.* It is a devotional practice in the Anglican tradition to read a Psalm in the morning and at night, and for me it is an experience of dipping into a well that is always full.

The Psalms enable me to see beyond my own circumstances because they show that the soul can indeed make contact with the outer world, even through and along with the process of vivid introspection. The consciousness of the Psalmist feeds on reality, a world in which God *is* and *reigns.* The poet's mind is at once inner- and outer-directed, as the Word of God was to the Hebrews—always active, having consequences in the real world.

In this way of wisdom, the opportunity for response is built in, the challenge to travel one direction or another, toward life or death, with one's whole being. Wisdom is the art of finding out what to do in the business of life. These ancient thinkers knew that no one can do it completely for another, give anyone else life prepackaged. However, their guidelines and reflections can help another approach decisions wisely—not as an utter fool who disregards the insight and experience of others.

How complex this way of truth is, living in wisdom. But we have yet to improve upon it as a way to live. The wisdom of the Psalms was given without complete revelation, before Christ's coming, but in it we find a mirror for souls in all ages.

Christin Other Guises

Let justice roll down like waters,
and righteousness like an everflowing stream.

C HRISTIANS OFTEN SPEAK of Christ's coming to us
in the guise of the stranger, the suffering, the needy,
but sometimes the seriousness with which we take this
notion is put to the test. Last night a desperate, incoherent
man called my husband here at the rectory; part of being
so public is having our home phone number listed in connection with the church. Apparently the man had tried
to persuade someone from a downtown Chicago church
to help him, but the season and the enormity of others'
needs at this time appeared to be working against him. Or
perhaps he had not heard what he wanted to hear from
whomever he had called earlier. The man said that if he
didn't get a favorable response *that night*, he would give up
on the Christ he had believed in for twenty-one years.

My husband has had this kind of urgent situation come
up before, and after listening to the man for a good twenty
minutes, decided this was one call he should not delay in
responding to—inconvenient though it was. I had very
mixed feelings, selfishly wishing my husband didn't have
to go out on a Friday night to an unknown situation in

snow that was steadily building into a minor storm. Since the man was downtown, a good forty minutes away on the breakneck Dan Ryan Expressway, I knew that for me it would mean a whole evening of waiting by the phone. He had agreed to meet my husband at the Greyhound bus station, not in the best of neighborhoods. He would let the man talk and give him what he had to give—his presence, backed by prayer, and enough money for a meal and a night's lodging.

Answering this cry required my husband to cancel a pastoral visit scheduled with parishioners in this nice, safe neighborhood, then go out to cash a check from his discretionary fund . . . and he was off into the thickening night.

I had just seen the weather report on TV and knew that a traveler's advisory was in effect, as the roads were fast becoming hazardous. How quickly and thoroughly I began to feel a lack of enthusiasm for this venture, I am ashamed to admit. I thought I was used to sharing my husband with needy and searching people, but it had rarely encroached on my convenience and fears for his safety as this incident did.

Was the request sincere? Or was the man dangerous? I began to pray as my husband left the house around 7:00, and I asked him to phone me as soon as he could tell me anything. He didn't call until around 9:30 and he was still downtown. All was well, he said; he had put the man up at the YMCA and given him enough cash to sustain him for the night. He had bought him a hamburger and had a long talk with him over the meal about what he could do to survive the next week. He was also going to get the man in touch with agencies that could help him further, now that the immediate crisis had been met.

I was relieved, although I knew that now it would take

at least another forty-five minutes for him to get home. So it was too soon to stop praying. I know these roads and our winters all too well, and the Dan Ryan is not the place to get stuck in an emergency. I felt alternately vulnerable and ashamed to be so weak in faith. I had thought I was ready for anything; parishioners have died in the middle of the night and my husband has had to rush to the hospital. Once he intervened in a marital squabble at 2:00 AM at the couple's request; the man had a gun and admitted he was not sober and needed help. Usually the presence of the clerical collar brings some sanity and equilibrium into crazy situations. And so does going out in the name and power of Christ. I often have to remind myself of that strength in order to assent to these crisis pastoral visits.

As my husband told me later, the man he went to see felt he had had "Christianity" shoved down his throat over the years, but had seen little of love tangibly expressed. In this situation he was deliberately putting the church on the line, either by chance or by providence asking my husband personally to fulfill a long-neglected need. It had been possible to reason with the man and pray with him, and mostly to listen. To this man *faith* had to be manifested in a real person willing to come out in a snowstorm, at some inconvenience and risk, to serve him that night.

Was it worth a trip to the city under these circumstances? We will never know—any more than anyone can measure the value of ministering to one soul. It is never convenient to have your belief put to the test, to have to make instant judgments of sincerity or foolhardiness. And when a request like this comes, it is always urgent, never offering you the luxury of time to decide beyond all doubt.

We never know how close to the edge another person

may be. One act of kindness could keep someone from slipping out of the reach of human love and mercy in the moment; words and acts might strike just the note that person needs to take the first steps across the precipice toward belief.

I have been reading in Amos of God's "wrath" against those who not only refuse to consider the poor and needy, but trample on their meager rights and turn them aside at the gate (Amos 5:10–12). This is a double offense, first of all to refuse hospitality to the stranger who comes to one's house; then to cheat him. In a time when there was always present danger from thieves and bandits, the offer of entrance to a home, a meal, and the chance to share safety and comfort was more than a mere nicety. And this rule of hospitality certainly has its parallel today, especially during winter in the city, as this man has just shown us. To welcome someone or turn him away at the gate—of one's house, church, or the "Y"—seems significant. Gates, walls, fences can open up to entrance or close one out from the security inside.

It seems that the needy come to us in the place of Christ himself, in the flesh, teaching us even in these early Old Testament passages that to value and preserve each other's flesh is a holy act. We have the chance to be "saviors" to others, literally, at crucial times when the needy person appears at our door. We always assume that we have ourselves to think of as well—our safety and that of our family. Is our own larder sufficiently full to last us? Have we already given "at the office" and do we feel overburdened by any further requests just now? We realize that we cannot throw money out into the street indiscriminately at the poor, lest we only show that we are fools, pushovers for a fast buck. There is a legitimate question of what to give to whom, and when.

Underlying the actual giving is the importance of our attitude, the way we approach our giving, rooted in justice and mercy:

> Let justice roll down like waters,
>> and righteousness like an everflowing stream.
> (Amos 5:24)

In teaching his disciples, Jesus made it clear that they always went out in his name to heal and preach:

> Whoever welcomes you welcomes me, and whoever welcomes me welcomes the one who sent me.
> (Matt. 10:40)

At the Last Judgment, Jesus teaches, the servants most faithful to him will be those who have fed and welcomed the poor just as they would feed and welcome him:

> For I was hungry and you gave me food, I was thirsty and you gave me something to drink, I was a stranger and you welcomed me. (Matt. 25:35)

I find it is much easier to talk about the ennobling aspects of the whole business now that my husband has returned safely and "met his obligation" for this particular man and his immediate needs. A little cynically, I wonder if the man will harass us or continue to ask for more support from the church funds. Although I believe in the healing power of love, applied as it is needed, I am also aware of the responsibility not only of those who give out of their bounty (which comes from God), but also on the part of those who receive.

Meditating on abstract concepts such as hospitality to the stranger is so easy compared to the reality knocking at your door or tying up your phone line, or posing any threat to your plans and carefully figured budget—of both time and money. It is in flesh that theology hits us hardest, in the implications and demands of Jesus' incarnation which reach to our very way of life and threaten our comfortable illusion of owning what we enjoy.

I remember well God's promise in the book of the prophet Malachi concerning tithing:

> Bring the full tithe into the storehouse, so that
> there may be food in my house, and thus put me
> to the test, says the LORD of hosts; see if I will
> not open the windows of heaven for you and pour
> down for you an overflowing blessing. (3:10)

The test of the stranger has roots in the story of Abraham's visitors at the tent who turned out to be angels unawares. It stretches through the Middle Eastern customs of hospitality that worked on earthly and practical terms, yet were also a spiritual duty. It is mirrored in the Good Samaritan, a picture of one's neighbor; and in Jesus' dependence on such a custom for the sending out of his own disciples, on whose survival and well-being the Gospel itself would hang. Care of the poor or temporarily needy, of the hungry and lost, is surely a sign of Christ himself, knocking and offering us an opportunity to put hands and feet on our belief. It is hard to see such things as offering a hamburger and a cup of coffee, an hour's silence of listening, and money for a night's shelter as welcoming Christ in another guise. But that is often exactly what we are asked to do.

A Wintry Spirituality

All weathers nourish souls.

*M*Y HUSBAND IS LATE getting home and we are expecting dinner guests in forty-five minutes. He has been at the wake of a young woman whose wedding he performed only last year. Several months later she discovered that she had cancer, and her condition began to worsen steadily. He has been in touch with her husband regularly, and now he is with the family.

It seems especially tragic to be burying a loved one in this season, this bleak and wintry time of pre-celebration. Surely it is an added dimension of grief knowing that the person who died will not be around for the days ahead.

Even though we all know that our days are numbered on this earth, some people seem more aware of the inevitability of winter in the soul. Somehow reflecting on this young woman's death draws my attention to lessons from the seasons about spirituality.

I have been reading Martin Marty's book *A Cry of Absence,* in which he discusses two basic types of spirituality: the summery and wintry modes of expression. He draws on some remarks in an interview with Karl Rahner, who saw the first or summery type as embodying the

enthusiastic, charismatic approach, "an almost naive belief in the immediacy of God and the power of the Holy
Spirit." Although he acknowledges the credibility of these
spiritual experiences, Rahner speaks also of the other type,
"a wintry sort of spirituality, in which [believers] stand
alongside . . . those who have perhaps excluded God from
their horizon." These wintry types, Rahner emphasizes,
are "committed Christians who pray and receive the sac-
raments," but their view accommodates the darkness and
the cold of silence in the soul.

Marty develops this extended view of wintry spirituality, particularly in relation to the Psalms, after noticing
that more than half the Psalms had "as their major burden
or context life on the wintry landscape of the heart. Many
more contained extensive references to the spiritual terrain
of winter, even if it did not predominate." This accommo-
dation of winter is surely an element in the Psalms that
has drawn me to them over the years, passages of troubles,
ponderings, and even the difficult imprecations against
enemies that seem so heartless and relentless (although as
a modern reader I tend to depersonalize those "enemies"
and turn them into adverse circumstances or projections
of my own failures).

Marty (as I do, I must admit) finds it easy to identify
with the wintry view, and considers it necessary to collect
and account for these negatives in the context of a positive
faith. I realize that my own perceptions of the nature of
life from earliest childhood fit most accurately into this
wintry view. No wonder Advent easily suggests itself to
me as a metaphor for all of life.

In the wintry type or style of spiritual expression, the
thought of death, the possibility of loss as an option, is

always present, if not predominant. One is compelled to keep believing through the snows of winter, the grayness—even to savor the bleakness for being exactly what it is, and therefore no pretense or false sign of hope.

For a wintry believer no summer day is ever without a reminder that this is not the condition one can expect of the whole year, certainly not in our Midwestern states (Marty also lives in Chicago). Yet the light and warmth of the sun are perhaps more fully appreciated because of their transience; the message they give to a wintry believer is that this ease is not to be relied on in the days ahead. Yet it is one of the gifts of a good God. Summer in its season has its lessons—and its perils, if its benefits should become necessary to sustain our faith. The wintry believer acknowledges rather that, as British missionary to India Amy Carmichael has said, "All weathers nourish souls."

Thus we are given days together with our loved ones, yet even their presence may serve to block our awareness of grace. It seems we cannot wholly appreciate presence *when we have it.* Perhaps, like nature itself, others are "too much with us." When all of life is too light, too full, we may be deceived into thinking we deserve its benefits and ease. Winter does not allow us that option. It is relentless, undeniable, in the world and in the soul.

Wintry spirituality is a kind of awareness, an acceptance of paradox—the coexistence of the irreconcilable. For the wintry believer, irony is a motif and a theme in our human story that cannot be ignored. Winter people know that even the most fulfilling presence of another is best mixed with a pinch of absence for contrast. The harder paradox is one of accepting that pain, too, has purpose and can be redemptive in the end; but our earthly life seems to teach us this.

Nostalgia for some lost state of perfection, for paradise, is certainly not lacking in wintry spirituality and may even be the stronger for its recognition of the fallen state of creation. Yet there is still the consolation of knowing that if such a place or state as paradise were possible here on earth, a sort of perpetual island retreat from winter, it would not further the nurture of the soul, and might even bring somnolence to the body and mind as well.

Exponents of wintry spirituality, like prophets of doom, are never popular because they are reminders of hardship and loss to unwilling hearts. When we see pain in the lives of others, or imagine possible scenarios of loss, we winter people too are scared. Yet those who know the wilderness of winter—an inner landscape without obvious relief—are allowed some glimpses in minute detail: of the hoarfrost of Psalm 147, frozen beauty as perfect as summer's master-pieces, an intensity of sun shattering the bleakness on un-expected afternoons, or the untouched beauty of "snow like wool" (v. 16) newly fallen. These can be reminders that "joy comes with the morning" (Ps. 30:5).

Some years ago I worked on a book with pediatric sur-geon Dr. C. Everett Koop, later the U. S. Surgeon General, recounting the death of his son David. Koop remarked that when he operated on impaired children and counseled their parents during the crisis, these couples often admit-ted that having a less than perfect child was the worst thing that had ever happened to them. Yet the resultant experi-ence of hope, trust, growth—often a turning to God—was also the best. No one would choose to experience winter in that way, through a child's suffering as well as one's own; but some who have traveled that way of bleakness report that even in it there is a way to live, to go on.

It is contemplating winter in the abstract that can paralyze. Facing any pregnancy, one can allow the mind to go crazy, imagining bizarre possibilities of what could go wrong. It is possible to go under just thinking of the vulnerable young life you have been given to raise, of the dangers of even ordinary existence—and of the grief we have already experienced, and the days of loss in our own families. It would be easy to fall into permanent deep-freeze, rather than merely to sustain awareness of the always-present possibility of winter.

If it is the danger of the summery spirituality to become superficial and appear naive, lacking credibility to a faithless world, then the temptation of the wintry person is to become morbid and jaded about the whole of life. Then one is unable to see even the good when it is given, like the dwarfs in C. S. Lewis's *The Last Battle* who are brought in to the marvel of the country of Narnia, with open sky and fresh flowers, but think themselves still in a dark, smelly hole of a stable. When given a feast of "pies and tongues and pigeons and trifles and ices," the dwarfs eat greedily but still think it to be stable food—"a bit of an old turnip" and hay and raw cabbage leaf. The rich goblets of wine in the kingdom they take for "dirty water out of a trough that a donkey's been at!"

Wintry believers must beware of seeing and tasting less than is really there for them. It is their task to bear in a prophetic way that "cry" of absence they have experienced—as a warning and reminder that there is more to life than the summer's ease. God has spoken to those of us in wintry straits, as often as not, in Scripture; its message applies to all conditions of souls.

Wintry people do not necessarily doubt or disdain the experience of summer as a metaphor for the Christian life, but interpret their own summer respites differently, coming to them with questions, perhaps with wistfulness and even envy that the landscape of their own hearts will never be so fair and light, their histories so unbroken by pain.

Yet there is a grim kind of comfort that the wintry person knows: When one has faced and survived one's worst nightmares, the terrors of the cold and the dark can no longer threaten in the same way. To emerge from the winter of the soul as still oneself, is to affirm the inherent goodness of creation, to validate life as it has been given. Though life is never again the same, it is wholly renewed.

From the vantage of winter, one can truly appreciate the "returns," the trips back to the solace of summer. In his poem "The Flower" George Herbert equates the return of spring with the renewal of fellowship with the Lord:

> How fresh, Oh Lord, how sweet and clean
> Are thy returns! ev'n as the flowers in spring;
> To which, besides their own demean,
> The late-past frosts tributes of pleasure bring.
> Grief melts away
> Like snow in May
> As if there were no such cold thing.

Novelists (such as C. S. Lewis in *Perelandra*) have posed the question as to whether a perfect, unfallen world is superior to one in which evil has already come, where the price has been paid, and all lies painfully in process of recreation to new glory. Are innocence and obedience superior to knowledge, to the drama of sin, fall, and rebirth? Reason says that poor means do not justify good ends, so the former must be superior. But the story we are in (as wintry believers will remind us) does not have the luxury of so simple a plot line. We are already in a more complex situation than we might wish. But if the winter person can remind us that God is present in the worst as well as the best of seasons, this too may save souls.

Those who have already taken into account winter's sting can experience a "second naiveté"; they can choose to go on with life. Wintry people are not as vulnerable to shock by the angry gusts from the north. If these people have a message for the world, especially for those who do not yet believe, it is the sign of their own continuing, pointing to the central paradox of the incarnation itself.

The widest of contrasts are embodied in the Christ child, as is so simply and profoundly expressed in the Richard Crashaw poem quoted earlier (page 15). He is the central figure of this season, toward whom winter longs and leans. At his birth we welcome

> Summer in winter, day in night,
> Heaven in earth and God in man!

Advent Three

Stir up your power, O Lord, and with great might come among us; and, because we are sorely hindered by our sins, let your bountiful grace and mercy speedily help and deliver us; through Jesus Christ our Lord, to whom, with you and the Holy Spirit, be honor and glory, now and for ever.

"Comfort Ye, My People"

I will shake the heavens and the earth
and the sea and the dry land.

TODAY WE ARE experiencing a break from some of Advent's soberness. It is Rose Sunday, the day when the pink Advent candle is lit and we remember John the Baptist through the words of Isaiah: he who saw that the entire world was a desert and a pathway had to be made.

We are looking forward to an afternoon of musical refreshment with our good friends in the parish, the Walkers. They have given us tickets to accompany them to Handel's *Messiah* and then are taking us out to dinner.

The Psalm that I read this morning sums up my need and my anticipation of this refreshment. Longing for more of God's presence is indeed like a thirst that cries to be quenched.

> O God, you are my God, I seek you,
>   my soul thirsts for you;
> my flesh faints for you,
>   as in a dry and weary land where there is no water.
> So I have looked upon you in the sanctuary,
>   beholding your power and glory. (63:1–2)

I, too, am entering a sanctuary this afternoon—the magnificent Rockefeller Chapel at the University of Chicago—in order to listen to the entire oratorio of Handel's *Messiah* at a fine level of artistry.

Simply entering the building itself is part of the replenishment I seek, even before the music begins to fill the sacred space with praise. The other people in the audience, the multitudes filling every seat and overflowing into the aisles, are part of this experience. Perhaps most of them have come only to hear a concert, the clean, bright sound of Handel's music indelibly wedded to a message they can either take to heart or perhaps revere as something out of the past, of antiquarian interest.

Yet for me, the people themselves have everything to do with the themes of this oratorio. It is about God's call to the nations, touching hearts through the Word, offering hints of a consummation in glory that lies ahead. To look at this crowd reminds me that our salvation is as much corporate as it is individual and personal. The stars, the sands, the branches of the tree are mirrored in these faces. Thus the comfort I seek—as one soul living through Advent, and as a woman experiencing the ordered months of a pregnancy—takes the form of promises that will hold for many others in their various situations, as well as for me.

As we settle in, not entirely comfortable in the hard seats, I prepare to allow the familiarity of the text and music work on me both in newness and in recollection of other times it has refreshed me.

"Comfort ye, comfort ye, my people, saith your God," it begins. I know that as the story told by Isaiah progresses we will need to return to that comfort promised by God. This is just the beginning of a story of redemption in which

we are all destined to be enfolded. We would do well to remember the underlying motif of God's love for us and
for creation, as the words and music draw us from these
thoughts of comfort to the bleaker texts of Jesus' Passion
and death.

I sense what is coming as the performance proceeds. The
oratorio tells the story of Messiah in the rich, descriptive
language of prophecy. The images, like those of all poetry,
both reveal and conceal at once. It takes ears to hear, eyes to
see, and time to discover what the Lord intends.

The Scripture text is not just beautiful poetry, although
it is that too. If we were to commission a poet to write epic
lines of a hero rising in a time of distress, and follow him
through a heroic chain of events, including thunderings
and reverberations in the heavens—one sent from a God of
might who reaches down to both *shake* and *heal* people—it
would be hard to improve on the epic that is *Messiah*.

The opening scenario, with God speaking, is startlingly
graphic:

> I will shake the heavens and the earth and the sea
> and the dry land; and I will shake all the nations,
> so that the treasure of all nations shall come.
> (Hag. 2:6–7)

I am reminded that the promises God gave to Abram, to multiply his descendants as the stars of heaven, were to be for
the blessing of *all* the nations (Gen. 18:18; 22:18; 26:4). Both
the music and the text of *Messiah* prepare us for God's
work to be accomplished on a cosmic scale. In Isaiah 40
we find the paradox of a God who views the nations as "a
drop from a bucket," and dust on the scales (v. 15); yet

God's concern for the individual is particular, caring, and tender, feeding the flock like a shepherd, and gathering the lambs in his arms.

This is to me another of the paradoxes of Advent, of God's coming into our lives in majesty, and with comfort as well. Jesus' earthly advent was shattering, earth-changing in its significance, not only for his people Israel, but for all nations and generations to come. He comes to "shake all nations," not for destruction, if those nations repent, but in order to get our attention. God uses a prophet such as Isaiah in his time and John in his time to prepare a way in the desert, a highway for our God. He acts as a king who has not forgotten his subjects, but needs to awaken and remind them of his present and future rule.

Where is comfort in the midst of this shaking and turbulence in the world of human beings? At that first coming, Jesus seemed to shake no one but a few local shepherds who, alongside Mary and Joseph, beheld him in weakness and at rest. Angels in glory, kings from the East, and presents befitting a king contributed to the contrasts of meekness and strength. But thirty years of a human life lived in ordinary time and place, with ordinary people, kept Jesus' might largely concealed.

Where was God's mighty arm then, the rule to break the Romans' tyranny over the Jews? Yet through Jesus *comfort was given,* the healing of people with whom he came in touch. "Peace I leave with you. . . . I am the good shepherd. . . ." The comfort of God came enclosed in flesh, more as a brother than a king.

This, too, is the hero we acknowledge in the majestic strains of *Messiah*: the Son of man.

Jesus' second coming is also hinted at in the oratorio, when the strands of might and comfort will be wound even tighter into the reality of a heavenly rule. In the words of human kingship and honor, wedded to the lowly image of Christ as Lamb of God, one with his sheep, we hear: "To the one seated on the throne and to the Lamb be blessing and honor and glory and might forever and ever!" (Rev. 5:13).

Experiencing the sweep of the oratorio—to this glorious conclusion, God's ultimate reign—offers me further glimpses of glory in Advent. The beauty of the promises, the catastrophic level of God's working among the nations—desiring both to *refine* and *comfort*—it is almost too much to bear. Perhaps it teaches me something of what our whole human life span is about, and some ways in which we too may become one with the mystery of God enfleshed.

We have come to look upon the Lord in the sanctuary, through the gift of music and prophecy that is *Messiah*. Now we leave the multitude, to go out in the fellowship of the particular friends who have shared with us this foretaste of glory. As we take up our own given lives at this point in the earth's turning, we are refreshed.

The Way of Silence

Silence, unless the reason for speech will bear the searchlight of Eternity.

ODAY, IN STARK CONTRAST to the experience of hearing *Messiah* in a cathedral filled with praise and people, I move back to the silence and solitude of my work.

Silence in itself is nothing foreign to me, and is in fact a welcome condition for meditation, for research, for thinking, and for allowing experiences to settle and be absorbed by the soul. It is not hard for me to practice silence—though I believe I am prepared to speak when the right questions are asked. Today I commit these words to paper in silence, but for the clacking of my typewriter. No one looks over my shoulder or directs me or asks me to do this work. I reflect not in a vacuum, but in the richness of silence. In fact, I perceive it as a *filled* silence, a phenomenon akin to active waiting.

> It is good that one should wait quietly
> for the salvation of the LORD. (Lam. 3:26)

As I look today at passages on silence in the Bible I cannot avoid being struck by Paul's injunctions in 1 Timothy where he tells women to keep silence in the sanctuary, to learn in silence. I did not want to deal with this, as it brings back childhood memories of being told that we girls were not ever to utter a word in a service. The one exception was that, upon joining the church, and being asked if you had accepted Christ, you could say "Yes." Yet women were allowed to sing solos—apparently a singing voice was different, and such an occasion did not leave any room for their own words to be uttered; they could not introduce themselves or say, "Now I am going to sing . . ." as men could. This was all only twenty or so years ago. I recently returned to my home church to find a woman standing up front at an easel giving a "chalk talk," but it was not on a Sunday or at a principal service, where I am told women still do not speak.

But the ban on my voice and those of other females must have made a deep impression on me, coming at such a young age. At the time I had no desire to say anything publicly anyway; I would have had no idea *what* to say. But nevertheless it set up a barrier in my mind and gave me reason to go inward, which was my natural tendency anyway.

Now, in my present situation, I want to offer silence as a gift, a seeming negation that points to a potential filling with Christ, whose voice is as the "sound of many waters." I know I am not ready for that voice in its musical fullness yet. The sounds of my own wants, questions, doubts run through my mind, filling me uneasily. I need first to experience a greater emptying.

My example for this emptying, especially in Advent, is not a woman, but a man. John the Baptist was known for his proclamation of Christ, not for his silence, yet in studying his life it becomes clear that silence and sureness girded up his message. There was something of silence about John the Baptist even as he spoke—something of self-limitation and renunciation of any claim to status. "He must increase, but I must decrease," he says of Christ (John 3:30). In Luke's gospel John proclaims his unworthiness: "One who is more powerful than I is coming; I am not worthy to untie the thong of his sandals" (3:16).

When John's message finally poured forth—"Prepare the way of the Lord; make his path straight"—the words were clear and focused. John spoke not falteringly, but with confidence earned in his own life of physical austerity in the wilderness, as he prepared for the role of friend of the Bridegroom. He was single-minded in his vocation, strong from the solitude of prayer and silence. When he broke that silence, it was only to reveal Christ.

It seems that we can only know this full silence, this close kin of *active waiting,* as we are willing to travel through the desert of our own lives, allowing ourselves to focus on Christ. It means permitting the winds and sands of normal life to strip away some of our fondest hopes, and especially our most treasured ideas about ourselves.

I see Advent as a season spent in the desert of waiting and silence, especially this year as I prepare for what will be the biggest change in my adult life: becoming a mother. I expect certain limitations will be set, as well as a greater realization of the balance of roles in my personal vocation. And for me, silence is a way of proceeding through the unknown territory ahead.

Because we have not told anyone yet of the coming birth, I am able to hold the word in silence. My pregnancy is of limited significance to others anyway. Friends will be happy for us. It will change my work situation somewhat, and this will affect a few other people. But inwardly, where silence resides, I expect personal growth and a hacking away at my self-occupation and selfishness built through the years of adult personal freedoms.

In silence, I ask for a deepening in preparation for the adjustments ahead; I also expect pain and weariness in the new demands, along with a stretching of my capacity for joy. Silence for a purpose, for a time, can be healing. If everyone would learn to practice a degree of silence—refraining from criticism that wounds, holding back when unsure how to proceed, praying behind the scenes without recognition, meeting one's own standards before expecting them of others—we would see, I believe, a springing forth of the benefits of silence. This principle holds on a small, local scale, such as in the parish; and in the wider arena of society at large.

C. S. Lewis, in his novel *Till We Have Faces,* warned that until we have gone through that natural process of purgation that is the tested life—including the desert—we will be compelled to offer God "the babble that we think we mean." And Amy Carmichael offered the principle of "Silence, unless the reason for speech will bear the searchlight of Eternity." Without a school of waiting, a discipline of silence, we are doomed to the insipidity and demands of our own voices, echoing solo in our narrow confines.

While I would not make too much of my own silence, I do see its value. Measured silence for a time is a gift, a privilege. I believe it can be as much a sign to the church and to the world as can teaching and preaching in their place. For me, silence through the desert of change is a way of working out my own salvation in fear and trembling.

The baby is silent in the womb, growing, changing, being nurtured, for that is the way new life is given. There is no choice but to submit to the natural process. All Christians too are dependent on the silence of the nurturing process of the Word becoming flesh in our lives. God speaks to and heals the inner person; yet we always hear and respond in the context of life, amid other voices and personalities. The outer cacophony can cause confusion, dim the inner hearing, or else provide a needed, contrasting background—context for our understanding and interpretation.

Silence for our souls, as for an unborn child, is a kind of limitation, yet I see it also as the necessary space that helps form the parameters of our life. Bernard Holland, writing of the importance of silence in music, says, "Silence is music's frame, its backdrop. It must precede music, underlie its progress and greet its end." The Book of Proverbs reminds me that words rightly chosen are "like apples of gold in a setting of silver" (25:11). Without the frame, the proper setting, the thing itself—painting, music, life—suffers lack of definition.

Knowing when to speak and what to say is as important and prophetic as silence in its time. Neither is better; one is useful for one thing, the other serves another purpose in the kingdom.

For now, silence is an old friend, a natural state to be in. To break it in good time is an occasion of grace. However, I wonder if any of us will ever be able, in this life, to speak much more than "the babble that we think we mean."

It is the Spirit's work to draw out that inner word in the fullness of time. Will God not bestow on each of us our own name, when our lives are able to embody it?

Royal Wedding

Heaven and earth are linked in a single bond, and the
world is a wedding.

I HAVE BEEN ASKED TO BE matron of honor in a
friend's wedding next spring, and—as so often hap-
pens with matrons of honor—I don't know what size I will
be by the time the date rolls around! My friend will be one
of the first people I will tell of my pregnancy.

It seems a little odd to be thinking about weddings in
Advent, as they are usually not performed in this season.
Yet in my readings of the Psalms today I came across an-
other reference to a wedding. Psalm 45 is a hymn sub-
titled "A Love Song," but instead I would title it "Royal
Wedding."

Perhaps some thoughts of weddings are not out of
place in Advent. Just as Richard Crashaw's poem "Welcome, All Wonders!" names the paradox of "Heaven in
earth and God in man," so Advent can be seen as an expectation of the wedding of heaven and earth in Christ.

I am reminded of an illustration from A. M. Allchin in
his book *The World Is a Wedding,* in which he describes an
instance of heaven and earth converging: A story is passed
on by a group of Celtic monks from the earliest days of the

order. It seems that none of the monks of this Celtic order ever died, even after old age set upon them. Eventually, in a vision, the monks were privileged to view an opening in heaven exactly the size of the monastery itself. In mythological language, this opening, with angels of God descending and ascending between heaven and earth, represented the idea of penetrating heavenly reality, tasting transcendence before one's time on earth is through.

In the story, once the monks realized the problem they moved their buildings to another location, the time-freeze was ended, and they were able to die after normal life spans.

Allchin comments that this story "is speaking to us in poetic language of the possibility that here in this world of flesh and blood men can realise, if only for an instant, the presence of the kingdom of eternity which is ever at hand, can recapture the innocence of the beginning and anticipate the fulfillment of the end. Heaven and earth are linked in a single bond, and the world is a wedding."

Far from having the problem of a too-intimate acquaintance with transcendence, most of us (unlike the monks) tend to miss the flashing instances of heaven touching earth, and we need to be reminded that the world is a wedding.

Advent expresses our anticipation of the wedding of heaven and earth; and by the brilliance of the image of such a consummation, all weddings derive some reflection of the glory.

A royal wedding such as is described in Psalm 45 also holds up the image of glory, in that it speaks of the marriage of the king himself. The psalm takes the form of a courtly eulogy of the wedding couple, and is an example of what we would call "golden poetry," rich in images and lustrous in descriptive language: glory and majesty, equity and righteousness, fragrance and gladness. The verses are devoted to lines in praise of first the king and then his beloved.

> You are the most handsome of men;
> > grace is poured upon your lips;
> > therefore God has blessed you forever.

> At your right hand stands the queen in gold of
> > Ophir.
> Her companions follow.

> With joy and gladness they are led along
> > as they enter the palace of the king.
> (vv. 2, 9, 14, 15)

Images of fruitfulness, of progeny to come, are here, too—the ultimate blessing on this union.

It is lovely poetry to read—especially aloud—but can we really claim for it any greater significance than a view of wedding customs in Israel and the interesting perspective of the Psalmist ready to record them: "My tongue is like the pen of a ready scribe" (v. 1)?

While it is important that we do not disregard the literal level of this psalm, it is not inappropriate for us also to think of the traditional image of God's union with the church as a kind of wedding. We are, in this day, quite wary of the dangers of flowery scriptural allegorization, the assumption that we can make a one-for-one identification of each detail with some hidden "spiritual" meaning. Yet we can certainly say that *any* wedding can tell us something about God's love.

J. B. Pratt has written that there are several reasons why the mystics have almost invariably used the language of human love and union in attempting to describe the nature of God's love. "The first and simplest is this: that they have no other language to use. . . . The mystic must make use of expressions drawn from earthly love to describe his experience, or give up the attempt of describing it at all. It is the only way he has of even suggesting to the non-mystical what he has felt."

Using words for divine ends can be a perilous pursuit, as language can be misunderstood. Any image can be taken for too complete an embodiment of what it merely represents. In her book *Travelling In,* Monica Furlong warns, "The saints often talk of God as a lover, and when they describe union with him they tend to speak (language cracking beneath their feet like rotten boards) in sexual metaphor."

The deeper we penetrate the mystery of romantic imagery, aware of both its usefulness and its limitations, the more we seem to be talking with an urgent but dying breath. To speak of the union of heaven and earth, or of any true union of opposites at all, when the world is impossibly broken, splintered, shattered, can seem naive at best.

But adopting the sexual metaphor of marriage does have a long history. This image is found in some of the greatest poetry in the Christian tradition, from the Song of Songs onward, and serves to balance out the Christian tradition of celibacy, so closely associated with pure devotion and dedication to spiritual ideals.

Both the union of bodies in marriage and the denial of sexual intimacy in the celibate condition can point to God as the giver of all good things, including the body and its potential for service. The apostle Paul writes of marriage as an analogy of Christ's love for the Church (consisting of individual souls; Eph. 5:22–33); and Jesus sometimes refers to himself as a bridegroom (Matt. 9:15). But these references could be spiritualized and used also as support for the *denial* of earthly marriage in favor of a mystical union with God. Therefore, it seems, Christian marriages that point to God's grace and are oriented toward ministry and a reflection of the good gift of sexuality can help to bring some balance to the issue.

Yet in our age it seems that the sexual metaphor, of which Dante in his time could speak without explanation or apology:

That hour when holy sorrow
Rewids the soul to God as his true wife . . .

is somewhat strained, in need of replenishment with instances of the reality it describes—if it is not to be disregarded altogether. At best, the image of marriage is still useful in the realm of poetic language. The ideals expressed in a wedding service can sometimes captivate national and international attention, and this is especially true of royal weddings. When they are focused on, the traditional vows of marriage seem to gather up their fullest Christian meaning, and can sometimes be born fresh in the media—in a world that now rarely considers the ideals of fidelity and longevity in marriage.

The Prayer Book words of the marriage ceremony are no less a "royal hymn" than the psalm before us. Of course, the special attention that royal weddings receive can make some people envious and angry. It's not fair; it's not equal.

Many worthwhile people do not receive the attention and good fortune they deserve. We could protest that various types of events are important to the world, and so why should this be given such attention? But the human interest in a royal wedding is sustained through all the objections.

The images of marriage and kingship, of course, are not representative of the totality, the fullness of what can be said of the workings of God's kingdom. Rather, Jesus in his parables used many analogies to expand language, urging us to see the kingdom also as a lump of leaven, a field, a woman with a coin. . . . Many types of human experience draw attention to God's workings: barrenness, silence, renunciation, bad kings and tragic marriages, prodigal children and faithless workers, grafted-on branches from which a next generation flowers.

If we begin with an acknowledgment of the frailty of language of any kind, I feel we need not be afraid to include all types of human experience in attempting to talk about God. Language is like a kaleidoscope, ever moving and changing, and we can at best catch a glimpse of an image as it is forming for us in the moment, before we move on. Yet I still enjoy this psalm and corresponding imagery in the Song of Songs: poetic reminders of the delight of human love, and certainly hints of even greater fulfillment in union with the Bridegroom who will come.

Royal celebrations may not speak to everyone of joy, unless it is remembered that we are all part of this court, and we choose to be drawn in to its life, or deliberately stand aloof and miss the festivities. The images are only a bridge to walk across, respectfully. Now we see as in a glass darkly; we won't need images forever. But even as we grow to see other facets and embrace other ways in the Spirit, we may feel a fondness for such signposts that got us to this point.

As I find myself in this journal talking of kings and weddings, I add these courtly images to the other signposts I value, those of growing things in the natural world: trees and fields, planting and harvesting, the death of a seed in the ground and the gift of light to quicken it, marrying and giving birth as the earth replenishes itself.

It is impossible in Advent, this season of the wedding of heaven and earth, to ignore the significance of the images of birth in God's plan. We *welcome all wonders,* including the miracle that flesh can bear God's image, can bear *God.* In one historic instance this was literally true. "For unto us a child is born, unto us a son is given." And God clearly endorsed this sonship: "This is my beloved Son, with whom I am well pleased."

The incarnation itself is the central event of the wedding of heaven and earth. How we sort out its images may depend on our personal inclinations toward or against the many types or signs of the kingdom offered to our senses.

In this psalm and at this moment, I celebrate the royal wedding. In the next, I remember the words of St. Thomas Aquinas: "Types and shadows have their ending when the newer rite is here."

Receiving the Gift

. . . the Holy Ghost over the bent
  World broods with warm breast and with ah!
    bright wings.

LAST NIGHT WE HAD A Eucharist and healing service at the church, after which St. Mary's Guild, a division of Episcopal Church Women, was to hold its monthly meeting. So in honor of that occasion, especially as it fits this time of the year, during the service we recited the Magnificat from Luke.

It is good to proclaim along with Mary, "My soul magnifies the Lord, and my spirit rejoices in God my Savior. . . ." To magnify is to intensify, laud, extol—to *enlarge.* Reflection on Mary, who has through the ages served as a picture of the soul in its openness to God, comes naturally in Advent.

She proclaims herself God's handmaiden, and offers herself to be acted upon by God in whatever way it takes to bring about the birth. Like a lover, Mary is not afraid to face the unknown, welcoming this child and all wonders into her life through her trust in her Lord.

The image of the soul awakening to God, as Mary awoke to promise, is a fine and rich model to explore, along with the active model of service. Her example makes it clear

that we are called in various modes, out of the very circumstances in which we find ourselves—whether boldly
to mold history by our acts, or to have such a gift of being
used by God unexpectedly thrust upon us.

In this waiting season of Advent, we are all Mary, receiving the unexpected gift of grace, unasked for, into our
individual lives. Bearing it may cost all that we treasure
and thought we couldn't live without. Echoing her "yes" to
God can be costly; but it is the path of life.

But in what sense does she "magnify"—enlarge—our
view of God? All our souls may be said to be receptive in
this particular way before God; thus examples of women
saints such as Mary are crucial in balancing out our view
of what it means to be a Christian. The Christian life is
not all activity, programs, plans. It also includes the solitude of waiting, of silence, so often associated with Mary.
Scripture speaks of our being clay and God being the potter. But even this image, when explored more deeply, can
yield some interesting twists.

Matthew Fox has said that "the potter not only pushes
the clay but is pushed by it." It seems that action is not
unknown even to such a seemingly inanimate object as
clay. Life itself is dynamic; it entails a pushing and tugging
between elements of reality, and nonetheless between the
soul and God. Is it possible that another paradox is present
here, in the models we have always taken to be opposites?

George A. Maloney, sj, believes that the soul's receptivity has other implications, that it actually reveals another
facet of the nature of God, besides activity in the world and
power over creation. Maloney seems to be saying that the
soul "magnifies" the Lord by its very nature—enlarges and
lauds as it mirrors the receptivity of God himself.

In *The Breath of the Mystic,* Maloney writes of God:

> If He is love, He is not only the aggressive Father
> who has first loved us, but He is also receptivity,
> He is also the *anima* who waits upon our return
> and then joyfully accepts our love.

Indeed, if receptivity is a good quality for the soul to have, where could it have come from but God? This is certainly not inconsistent with the picture we get in the parable of the Waiting Father and the Prodigal Son. The Father waits and receives, not out of weakness, but in strength. This too is a challenge to the soul, another shade of the many images that point toward, but fall short of, describing God in totality.

This image of the soul as mirroring its Creator through receptivity also has implications for a greater appreciation of Mary and other feminine models of the soul. It suggests a respect for feminine richness and abundance. If God is the Pursuer, God is also the Divine Fullness the soul longs for, the eternal rest before which all our frenzied activity seems mere child's play. In the face of that plenitude, that quality of rest, the soul can seem, for an instance, in a mystery, almost an initiator, a seeker toward God.

C. S. Lewis, in his novel *That Hideous Strength,* makes the case through the use of hierarchical imagery that God is so masculine that we are all utterly feminine in comparison. Lewis's view is jarring at a time of emphasis on the feminine qualities of God in current theological work. Yet his analogy can be seen simply as one side of a two-faced coin. The flip side, while it seems harder to get at (and we must rely as always on images to do so) seems to imply that God must *also* be so "feminine" that we are all "masculine" in comparison.

I believe that resistance to the use of feminine imagery and pronouns for God is due to subtle inferences that such language may be somehow better or more "with it," or a necessary replacement for the tired masculine terminology we have taken for granted in describing God's nature. But solely to substitute feminine terms would be to fall prey to a newer, fresher idolatry—unless we again see language as that kaleidoscope that offers one picture, then fades into another, no single image holding the truth for long without qualification, alteration, correction.

In the case of masculine and feminine imagery, we can't avoid looking to our human experience as male and female and drawing specific applications. But it is also important to remember that men and women contain both masculine and feminine traits within them, and whether we employ a masculine or a feminine model, the soul will find something with which to identify. Though he uses a masculine construct, C. S. Lewis also wisely points out that "obedience and rule are more like a dance than a drill—specially between man and woman where the roles are always changing." He later wrote of his wife (in *A Grief Observed*) that Solomon called his bride "sister," but in some moments and moods a man is almost tempted to call her "brother." Marriage and friendship, sexuality and comradeship in a mature relationship, such as he and his wife had, can bring—not necessarily confusion—but a richness of overlapping truths.

Even though—perhaps because—I am a woman, it has

taken me some time to become comfortable with feminine images of God. I was used to thinking of God as Shepherd, King, Father, Husbandman, Bridegroom—acting upon the soul in its awakening, guiding its stages of obedience and action. These images imply a masculine shaping of the cosmos as well as a power over the soul—a Being overwhelming in force and effect, transforming the soul forever. Yet I was pleased and surprised some years ago to begin discovering and also incorporating into my thinking some powerful feminine images of God. One in particular was quite astonishing: the name for God, *El Shaddai*—*El* meaning God, and *Shaddai* coming from a root meaning "breast":

> By the God [*El*] of your father, who will help you,
> > by the Almighty [*Shaddai*] who will bless you
> > with blessings of heaven above,
> blessings of the deep that lies beneath,
> > blessings of the breasts [same root as
> > *Shaddai*] and of the womb. (Gen. 49:25)

Some of the work being done in feminine imagery takes into account qualities of God the Holy Spirit which coincide with feminine gifts and nurture. For instance, in Genesis 1:2 there are hints of God the Holy Spirit's presence at the very gestation of the worlds: a mighty wind that "swept over the face of the waters." Poet Gerard Manley Hopkins, in his poem "God's Grandeur," captures some of this feminine creativity in his lines:

> Oh, morning at the brown brink eastward,
> > springs—

Because the Holy Ghost over the bent
World broods with warm breast and with ah!
bright wings.

This image is also reflected in Jesus' longing to gather the children of Jerusalem under his wing like a mother hen (Matt. 23:37).

Women need to explore these and other images in Scripture and poetry in order to further appreciate their own nature, to recognize their receptivity, their unique ability to bear and nurture children, as part of the nature of God. Sister Penelope, friend of C. S. Lewis and author of *The Wood*, a book that treats major themes in Scripture, writes that the "Spirit 'was moving,' or rather 'was brooding,' over the face of the primeval chaos, as if it were hatching something out of it."

We need these stronger feminine images of God found in Scripture, such as a fire cast upon the earth (Luke 12:49) and the mighty rushing wind of the Spirit (Acts 2:2). While we can't speak of God the Spirit in the incarnate sense that Christ became a man, these realizations of the feminine side of Godhead help put some of woman's own nature into proper perspective, as valuable and rooted in God.

If the roles between man and woman are more a dance than a drill (ideally, as joyful lovers can attest) the relationship between the soul and God is also more of a flow in which grace and human choice, unmerited favor and our own will, act together in concert: in coinciding channels rather than separate connections. Gregory of Nyssa writes: "When righteousness of works and the grace of the Spirit come together at the same time in the same soul, together they are able to fill it with blessed life."

This is not meant to equate the creature with the Creator on equal terms; we always admit, as humans, that "we give thee but thine own." Our ability to give is itself a gift of God. But it does remind us that receptivity is a quality both of the soul and of God.

As I reflect on my present participation in these mysteries, through the work of preparing for birth, it is wonderful to acknowledge that my physical state of pregnancy, together with the conditions of my mind and spirit, can magnify my Lord, reflect the divine nature, give forth praise to my Creator.

As women seek to understand and live in the power of their innate receptivity, in sexuality, conception, and receiving a child to nurture, it is another way of tasting the blessedness of Mary and her soul's desire to magnify her Lord in her condition as handmaid.

Receptivity in this season, for men and women alike, surely can be expressed in many ways. It is echoed in the words of any soul, in any state, that will implore, "Come, Lord Jesus . . ."

Fire and Wind

Our God comes and does not keep silence.

*A*FTER CONTEMPLATING the themes of silence and receptivity, it is fitting to come to Psalm 50 this morning and encounter the other side of the coin. This psalm speaks of God's action and might, biblical images of power, the strength of God's voice in the world.

> The mighty one, God the LORD,
>> speaks and summons the earth
>> from the rising of the sun to its setting.
> Out of Zion, the perfection of beauty,
>> God shines forth.

> Our God comes and does not keep silence,
>> before him is a devouring fire,
>> and a mighty tempest all around him. (vv. 1–3)

We know that the fire and tumult of God's nature are part of Advent thinking as well, along with the silence, the waiting. The coming of Christ to his people, the experience of God-with-us, has its dramatic side; it is like thunder in the heavens in its impact on the world, pronouncing a new development in the redemption of creation.

What are some of the implications of God's powerful voice for our own proclamation of the Word? I have come from a tradition in which visiting evangelists always stressed the importance of boldness in witness; yet despite the loudness of their voices, they all said pretty much the same words, even to the point of cliché. There was forcefulness, but to my mind little real power.

As I began to grow into adulthood, I found myself searching for ways of passing on God's Word in forms that would reflect integrity in my *own* experience of God's coming into my life. I had a desire for the fresh wind of the Spirit to blow upon me, to clear away triteness and the hollowness of words that did not spring from my own understanding, but were merely warmed over for reuse. Becoming a "witness" was not the easy thing for me that it seemed to be for others, as I read of God speaking in many ways, some apparently contradictory: in a mighty voice; out of a whirlwind; and in a still, small whisper. Though I never lost the desire or even the urgency of proclaiming what I understood of God and God's ways, I found myself mostly "in school"—learning how to listen and being taught by teachers both living and dead, from the pages of books and by life itself. I discovered in myself a need for greater and deeper humility, before attempting to speak or write anything at all. And I discovered more and more aspects of the wonder of language, as it is able to convey the nuances of spiritual life and its consequences. Along with this came realization of the incredible *limitation* of words.

The task of presenting one's spiritual insights to the world, in the tradition of Scripture and its language, is clearly not one to be trusted to clichés and secondhand usages. It requires one's whole being and life as a sounding board and a vehicle of expression. When I first discovered John Donne's bold lines, "Batter my heart, three-person'd God," I realized I had come full circle to experience the forcefulness of encounter with God linked up with the true power of creative expression. It was not difficult to "intuit" meaning, to connect it with my own desire for God to invade and reconstruct my own life with whatever might be required to make me usable, with integrity. Yet even the power of expression of those lines is wrapped in the art of poetry. What if we do not have ears to hear?

What a risk God takes in trusting the frailty and the personal inclinations of human vessels to pass on understanding! I believe God does honor a desire for authenticity and appropriateness of our speech and action. Yet sometimes it takes years for the Word to take root and grow quietly, before it is reborn in an individual soul and starts to push above ground in something we might call ministry.

Today it is no surprise to me that I have ended up in a church in which language is valued and regarded on its own terms, along with the creative arts that both use words and render words useless. We have respect for visual and verbal (and other) channels that convey truth, and in the Episcopal Church I find space to grow and learn. It is wise to realize that human beings need intellectual freedom in order to act with true moral integrity. This freedom to think while practicing my faith allows me both to drink deeply of tradition and to live fully in my own time, which desperately needs to have wisdom conveyed in modes it can understand and value.

Yet people learn and listen in different ways. While I have leaned toward the poetic, subtler arts of uplift, enlightenment, and persuasion—without which I would have been, for all practical purposes, lost—others seek a more broadly proclaimed voice of an evangelist or lifestyle movement. The images in today's psalm, of God coming in the company of a devouring fire and a mighty tempest, allow room for both interpretations. Fire in the individual soul, and its expression of God's nature and work, is merely a microcosm of that larger sweep, which we might call "revival."

Despite my own affinity for the inner, the personal, I am growing to see how much we need both, and how those who work with language, with consciousness, can contribute to the clarity of the "trumpet call" of redemption when it does ring out in the world.

Today, literal fire-and-brimstone preaching is less popular; but the images of God's might are never hackneyed or trite. The openness and ambiguity of such biblical images as fire can allow replenishment of the message along with a return to its meaning for individuals. For instance, fire has its healing as well as its terrible aspects. In George MacDonald's fantasy, *The Princess and Curdie,* Curdie is admonished by the wise old princess to thrust his hands into a fire of burning roses, which smell sweet but are never consumed. Though the pain he experiences is intense, his hands emerge undamaged—and in fact, made smooth and refined, "knowing and wise." Enduring the fire is ever an image of the phoenix, of rebirth.

Images such as fire are concrete instances of the transcendent. Without such a vision the people perish, whether in Old Testament times when the cloud of God's presence and the pillar of fire led the way for Israel, or today, when some individuals and movements still image forth fire in words and actions.

Sometimes it takes the intensity and danger of fire truly to accomplish God's work. At the coming of the Spirit on the day of Pentecost, power was manifested at the sound of a mighty wind, and flames of fire like tongues rested on the heads of the apostles as they were gathered together in one place. Through this gift they were enabled to spread their ministry abroad, and their work in discipling nations became a fire cast upon the earth, as though blown by a wind, gathering all in its wake—unstoppable, changing history.

The work of the artist, too, has often been equated with a visitation of power, a gift of the spirit, the inspiration of the muse. Fire and wind must arise from somewhere; when they touch a receptive soul, they result in action and power. Sometimes the force of artists' best work is known only locally, while some poetic voices, such as Annie Dillard's, are able to direct a profound message to a wider audience. In *Teaching a Stone to Talk,* reflecting on God's wonders in the world and in our lives, she writes,

> God does not demand that we give up our per-
> sonal dignity, that we throw in our lot with random
> people, that we lose ourselves and turn from all
> that is not him. God needs nothing, asks nothing,
> and demands nothing, like the stars. It is a life
> with God which demands these things.

Dillard earns the right to say what God is like, and what the Transcendent does or does not demand, through the integrity of her life and work as a thinker and writer. Her writing reflects a life of searching and finding enough of the truth to be able to live.

When our language is strong and accurate, especially when it considers God's work through the ages, in Scripture and in the lives of other saints, it *is* a fire in the world, and cannot help but burn and heal and spread. Words fitly spoken, especially those that we dare to utter about God, will have a respect for their audience and allow for the dignity of an honest response, whether in contemplation or action. Words that finally come, after the inner growing season, are like a filled silence, action that redeems in the fullness of time.

How important is the individual bearer of fire today? Just as icons are now appropriate in visual art, since Christ's coming, so the significance of the individual bearing his image is also of great import. Whereas, according to Scripture, in Old Testament times the multitudes were able to see God's mighty acts and hear God's voice in thunderings and fire upon the mountain, today such manifestations seem subtler, more diversified, penetrating many areas of life.

While sermons and impassioned speeches have had some effect on me, it is in the quieter witness of novels such as François Mauriac's *Vipers' Tangle* and Charles Williams's novels—showing doctrine in action, a world in which heaven and earth interpenetrate—that I have been especially touched with fire and heard God's voice, changing my life forever.

Artists and writers who have spoken authentically and powerfully from the depth of their faith have quickened my own belief, spread it into my life and the lives of others, and thus multiplied their witness. Their use of language in a blend of freshness and tradition has also enabled me to return to Scripture with new eyes. Turning to poetry and fiction in the Christian tradition has made me appreciate the continuity of revelation, of God's conversation with the human race, from which the powerful symbols and themes of faith have arisen. I have needed to discover in the writings of other believers examples of the fleshing out of faith, particularly of doctrine, in a way that had integrity for me.

In the arts it is harder to judge whether the note is being sounded clearly, whether the words are read and heard, whether they fall on deaf ears or any ears at all. Such are the risks of the flame of fire within, as it enters hearts and spreads upon the earth from person to person.

This Advent I look to Scripture, to the majesty of prophecy and the glory of the Psalms, the message of the gospels and epistles, to stir up my own heart to hear God's voice in the world and respond in this present moment. Advent is a unique opportunity to proclaim that God has spoken, is speaking, and will speak in might to reveal not only *Christ among us,* but ourselves *to* ourselves, and what is required of us as part of the chain of witnesses to his power.

Redeeming Time

Time, unredeemed, is death's dominion.

$\mathcal{T}$ODAY IS MY BIRTHDAY. My parents came in from the suburbs to see our house for the first time and take us to lunch in the neighborhood; then we gave them a tour of the church and showed them more of our area by car.

It was a fitting, low-key way to spend the day. I don't think of birthdays as having much impact on me, except cumulatively. Before the actual day itself—months ahead—I tend to start thinking that I am already a year older. Perhaps I am unconsciously accommodating the change gradually, so the day itself *can't* undo or startle me. But the result of this is that I often don't remember how old I really am.

Yet writing about the occasion of another birthday does make me philosophical. If this were the last day of my life, rather than the beginning of a new year, I could say I have lived much as I wanted to, that life so far has been richer than I could have imagined, and already more terrible than my worst dreams.

It is hard to see your own span of time in any accurate perspective, because you can't step out of it to look back objectively; whatever you do becomes part of that span!

C. S. Lewis once wrote that we must not be destined always to live in time, because time seems so strange an environment to us. Imagine fish that were constantly amazed at the wetness of water! Their amazement might indicate, he suggests, that they were destined one day to become land creatures.

Yet though we sense ourselves destined for something, somewhere else, we are rooted in our own time, expected to make good of its raw material, which is its moments. We strive in vain to capture it as it flows like water through our fingers. A better response is to drink deeply of time and live off the gifts of life, day to day. Becoming one with our own time is the only way to redeem it.

Virginia Stem Owens in *And the Trees Clap Their Hands* writes of the tragedy of growing up and forgetting our mission, losing sight of the Jerusalem whence we have come: "Instead of colonizing time, instead of becoming a funnel through which Time flows into Eternity, [man] is himself colonized, devoured by time. And time, unredeemed, is death's dominion." She senses that we are all meant to be—if not prophets, at least witnesses and builders—colonizers of God's kingdom. And that mission is bounded by our earthly life span.

Along with my remembering birthdays and the flow of time (through me, as I am a funnel, a channel to the next generation; around me, as I am immersed and rooted in time), I'm sure I am forgetting much as well. As the years pass, youthful goals become entities in themselves rather than means to wholeness, to service; sometimes I forget simply to look and listen, the most elementary instructions to follow on any journey. But we always think we are somehow different from those who have gone before, despite their warnings, their wisdom. We expect that we will be able to go against the common grain and redeem *our* time.

The New Testament writers warn believers to make the most of time—to "redeem" it—because the days are evil (Eph. 5:16; Col. 4:5). This implies that there is a way to squander what span of time we are given, a way to refuse to be that funnel connecting ourselves to others and to eternity as links in the kingdom. To ignore this responsibility would be to deny the overlapping of God's time and our time, the miracle of "eternity shut in a span," visible and incarnate, drawing us to its center—to deny that Christ, God With Us, ever came.

We may say we believe in the incarnation literally, but I wonder how we might have reacted to Christ's physical presence had it been manifested within our time span. It was hard for Jesus' contemporaries to accept his oneness with God, to see him as any different from the other prophets who came along periodically. How could it be possible in *their* time that Messiah would appear in the flesh?

Israel had longed for that One who would come to redeem time, end exile, and become a bridge to peace. If, as someone has said, Isaiah 53 was advertising for a Messiah applicant, one who would suffer to redeem his people Israel, Jesus certainly fulfilled the requirements. But he did not openly hand out his résumé. Instead he *spent* his own life as an answer to any challenge to his identity. In Matthew 11 he "answered" the disciples of John the Baptist with enigmas and questions rather than with clarification. Jesus asked them to look at the evidence themselves: "The blind receive their sight, the lame walk, the lepers are cleansed, the deaf hear, the dead are raised, and the poor have good news brought to them" (v. 5). He says, "Let anyone with ears listen!" (v. 15).

Jesus' life and death are our prime example and form the key to redeeming time. He lived fully and humanly, as well as sacrificially, in his own time. His call for us to have listening ears and observant eyes implies more than sharply tuned faculties. Desire for service to the kingdom must lie behind our openness to phenomena. We live in expectation that the moment we are in may require something of us, may draw us into the vortex where we will lose whatever control over ourselves and our time we thought we possessed.

By our desire to redeem time we open ourselves to the flash of insight that makes us see our slice of reality in a different light. We are moved not by a meaningless flow of moments, but by our understanding, to see that eternity interpenetrates the stream of time in which we are immersed.

John the Baptist saw his own time and his mission as overlapping with the kingdom of God, so much so that he appeared and sounded ever the fanatic. He too fulfilled a "job description": "See, I am sending my messenger ahead of you, who will prepare your way before you" (v. 10). "If you are willing to accept it, he is Elijah who is to come" (v. 14).

Does that much really depend on our human response? Is prophecy fulfilled, and the time made the most of only when we affirm that "today it is fulfilled in our sight"? John was a funnel, connecting those he baptized to eternity through his faithfulness to the Word. He came proclaiming, "Repent, for the kingdom of heaven is near." Indeed, it was everywhere at hand, as close as touch and human assent. He was a redeemer of his time, the voice of one crying out in a wilderness of forgetfulness.

As he baptized in the Jordan, John carried out a rite that was reminiscent of the cleansings of Old Testament law, but its vital and graphic earthiness became fresh in his time. He was both foreshadowing and participating in the coming baptism of Christ, a renewal of spirit and of fire. We may see baptism as a kind of housecleaning, the beginning steps of the kingdom's work to clear the threshing floor and gather up the wheat to honor and the chaff to destruction. How odd that lines of eternal destiny could be equated with such physical acts. What a fair warning God gives of the consequences of blindness, deafness, sloth, hardness of heart.

Jesus began his public ministry by putting his endorsement on this ritual, undergoing it himself at John's priestly hands, bringing new meaning to an ancient rite of cleansing; redeeming and making it new in his own time. What bold strokes of the kingdom's outline are traced by the lines of baptism: acts in time, for their own sake and as a dramatic demonstration to a people bound up in custom, while forgetting the purpose of it all, the hope of redemption.

The figure of the Baptist as a redeemer of time helps me to see how many threads of God's purposes are pulled together in the advent of his Son. John, as a prophet in his own time, is also a link to our time, through his message of repentance and preparation that still echoes in the world. The odds were against anyone such as John appearing on the scene at all. He was born in a most unlikely way, to parents beyond child-bearing years: a woman hoping her time of fertility could yet be redeemed, and a skeptical husband. Out of pain and thwarted hopes, John sprung, a picture of the incarnation (as we all are), cast into a world of unbelief, dead wood, fear, fuzziness of vision. He was a man who dressed and ate in uncommon ways, willing that his very body be a sign, his life a funnel.

We can't do much about the time we are born into; we can take neither credit nor blame for the pluses and minuses of our heredity, our given circumstances. But we can look around us and seek to make the most of the time allotted to us, be willing to bear the mark of a prophet, be a witness to God's message in whatever way we are called. But, but, but, we say. . . . There are always extenuating circumstances, legitimate excuses. Not many of the prophets have seemed naturally suited or inclined to their tasks. Think of Jonah or Jeremiah.

The colonizing of the kingdom, building up the city of God as witnesses and workers, will cost us our lives. In whatever sense we find ourselves called to give them, it is also the only way to redeem them.

The Banquet

All the world is one great sacramental loaf.

WE FINALLY GOT OUR Christmas tree up, in time for the open house that we are having for the parish tomorrow. It started with a mishap. We had left it soaking overnight in a pail of water on the porch, and the water froze. So we had to bring in the unwieldy tree, put towels under it, and let it thaw before we could raise it.

Our seven-month-old kitten has discovered that a Christmas tree is a toy designed for him. Ornaments on lower branches are a constant temptation to his curious nature. It is amazing to imagine that next year we will be introducing our own child to the lights and splendor of Christmas.

The house is festive now with candles in all the windows, a large wreath over the fireplace, and familiar seasonal touches around the room that have now been added to the Advent wreath. We are preparing for a supper, our yearly open house for parishioners and other friends.

Right now I feel only tired, and I read, "Cast your burden on the LORD" (Ps. 55:22). As our waiting and watching for the Lord's birth is drawing to an end, we find ourselves taxed by the demands of daily life, tempted to let up on our

watch, go lax in our work. But the challenges we are facing won't allow for sloth or indifference. At this time our
prayer for our own flock is for unity.

Even in the church we are reminded that there are always differences, divisions. Not everyone desires oneness,
and we ourselves struggle with the cost of the unity for
which Jesus prayed. The letter of Jude says that there will
be scoffers in any age—people who cause divisions. It calls
those who deny authority and rebel "blemishes on your
love-feasts" (v. 12). Harsh words for what sometimes seem
to be petty differences among us, yet these words are especially relevant as we act out a tableau and symbol of
unity—the banquet.

> Build yourselves up on your most holy faith; pray
> in the Holy Spirit; keep yourselves in the love of
> God; look forward to the mercy of our Lord Jesus
> Christ that leads to eternal life. (vv. 20–21)

We are waiting for Christmas; but even after it comes
we will still be waiting for eternal life in the unity of the
kingdom. There is a way to live in any time of unbelief,
of divisions. There are some in the church who threaten
to separate themselves. Several divorces are pending as
couples try to get through this family season. Other people
seem to practice constant dissatisfaction and spread it into
others' lives. Rebellion exists in families, in nations. Yet we
give to the Lord that burden, the fear of disunity. And we
are learning to become expectant for God's mercy in this
place, at this time—as we pray and work for peace and the
healing of hearts.

We are to "have mercy on some who are wavering," Jude

goes on to say, and even to save some by "snatching them out of the fire" (vv. 22, 23). The fires of loss, division, loneliness may be closer than we think. When the self and self-gain becomes all one desires, hell reigns in the heart already.

We want to stand against the cold, to bring people in. To keep our table replenished, our doors open, requires faith. I need a vision; God's people need a vision, even as we practice our faith and worship together regularly. Without continual reminders, attention-getting flags of Scripture and liturgy, we have no hope of staying alert hosts. I know at least that we can't bring about unity by ourselves. It is hard enough to hold together—hence the deadliness of division; and it is almost impossible to hold on to truth, to vision, singly. We are too easily distracted, fooled, lulled by self-interests. None of our hearts is wide enough to contain the truth; it can become distorted so quickly without the checks and balances of each other's conscience and consciousness.

For our local community of faith, this Christmastide, I long for unity, for a lifting of the heaviness of self-concern that weighs us down. I see the effects of strain, of hopes thwarted for many. We must learn to live in the day, in the Light, even before we feel its warmth and power. The message to us all in our weariness and strain is, "Come to the banquet which is prepared for you." Our Lord is willing, offering himself in delight and replenishment for our bodies, our souls. Our planned supper is a small offering toward unity, fellowship, healing, intending to offer a pleasant stop on the way to the real banquet.

I look for some strengthening of the Body through this time of fellowship at our house. It is important to us that people feel welcome in the rectory, that it be a center of hospitality and friendship and refreshment of spirit. This open house offers us an opportunity to give back something of what has been provided for our family by so many. During our marriage we have held such an event every Advent about this time, but this will be the first in this parish. We know that small meetings will go on in different corners of the rectory, between people who might not talk to each other anywhere else.

It will be a feast, a banquet of sorts. We do not expect to regulate its flow, but simply to provide opportunity for hospitality, for the Spirit to break down barriers in this season of expectancy and hope. We ask for reconnection for those who still feel themselves to be on the outside; for deeper giving and more love among those on the "inside"; for people to see new sides of old personalities, and acknowledge the ways other people uniquely reflect Christ. "Look on others and not just on your own things," the apostle Paul said.

For us, this banquet is a type of the kingdom: beckoning, drawing in, feeding. The candles placed in the windows are hints of warmth and welcome. We have cleared a path through the snow to the doorway. As the door swings open again and again, with greetings and huggings, the many fragrances of food waft out from within, and sounds of friends' voices can be heard from adjoining rooms.

We are all in rehearsal for that great banquet to come, the Supper of the Lamb. Through simple choices of unity over division, kindness over bitterness, prayer over anger, we do help to usher in the kingdom, prepare the way, call attention to the Good News. Eating and drinking together has everything to do with joy, with the destiny for which we were created, as Jesus has reminded us again and again.

"All the world is one great sacramental loaf," writes Virginia Stem Owens. "We are not—nor will we ever be, God save us—solitary intelligences spinning in the dark void of space. . . . Creation is a birthday gift for the Son. . . . He hides in the bushes, jumping out in flames to startle us into seeing. He sequesters himself in stables and swaddling so as to take us unawares. He veils himself in flesh."

He is here, will be here in our mix of people. His work is in flesh—in the multitude of gifts and needs represented, a true picture of the kingdom. He longs to wake us up, to draw us to himself—to make us citizens of his city through the operations of love, which extend even to our doors and streets. We are practicing the unity of fellowship best when we allow the Spirit to grant us sight, to enable us to look on others without envy, to allow ourselves to become one with others and with him.

Today I am immersed in the mundane circumstances of the banquet—the everyday level of human preparation. And afterward there will be the inevitable crumbs, the drops spilled, perhaps a broken lamp, knocked down by an errant elbow, scattered needles from the tree, the cold pouring in from outside at each departure. All could distract, dull our vision of his presence.

But for now the lights still burn in the darkness; the gifts of food and drink are a breaking of that sacramental loaf, which we offer to each other as wine of the Spirit, nourishing to body and soul.

Advent Four

Purify our conscience, Almighty God, by
your daily visitation, that your Son, Jesus
Christ, at his coming, may find in us a man-
sion prepared for himself; who lives and
reigns with you, in the unity of the Holy
Spirit, one God, now and for ever.

A New Thing

Flesh knows what spirit knows
but spirit knows it knows.

$\mathcal{F}$ATIGUE AND THE NEED for a blood-sugar test sent me back to the doctor yesterday. This week I am to rest more, put my feet up, and watch my diet carefully.

The intrusion of physical changes is a reminder at this point that something is really happening to me. Pregnancy is not an idea but a reality. It is an experience about which we can reflect and draw conclusions, make comparisons to the spiritual life, as I am doing in this journal. Yet at the same time it remains a condition in itself, not a metaphor. Pregnancy is rich and complex and transformative—it does not need to be "elevated" to be of value.

Part of me facetiously wonders what it does to my state of mind to elevate my feet while reclining. "Favoring" a member is a clear indication that all parts of the body deserve their due, have their place in the natural scheme. Each physical change puts the mind–body problem in a different perspective—especially for someone who has always revered mental activity and seen it as paramount, closer to the spiritual life. I am increasingly aware that this bias itself can border on idolatry.

My experience as a woman right now helps elucidate for me a phrase from Charles Williams's poetry that until now I have always experienced intuitively: "Flesh knows what spirit knows / but spirit knows it knows," from *The Region of the Summer Stars.* The body has its own virtues and needs, and its own dignity in creation. It is wiser than we sometimes give it credit for being, and its life overlaps the spirit's—"coinheres," as Williams would say. Undoubtedly, following the doctor's advice is as important for the wholeness of my spirit as it is necessary for my body.

God is doing a new thing in me this Advent. It is so clearly indicated by changes in my body, but it also involves my intellect and will at every point. In the passage from Isaiah I am reading, chapter 42, God promises deliverance and justice to the faithful—a physical as well as a spiritual release. The deliverer himself is flesh and blood: God's servant. A new page is unfolding in the fulfillment of God's covenant with the people, and the new turns are an outgrowth of this people's history as a nation: "I have taken you by the hand and kept you . . ." (v. 6) like a parent who prevents separation and danger. The prophet declares,

> See, the former things have come to pass,
>   and new things I now declare;
> before they spring forth,
>   I tell you of them. (v. 9)

God the Father gives "breath to the people . . . and spirit" (v. 5). From God's hand comes the gift of life, as it was first breathed into Adam—but with even greater intention now, to include also the spiritual. In these lines of poetry and prophecy is an exquisite interface of the physical and the spiritual in one thought. Breath is part of our bodily functioning as human beings; spirit is an unseen part of our being, the soul's "breath." Respiration itself is a hint in our physical makeup that we are more than the tangible, measurable composite of bones and flesh. Our breath flows from physical organs, but is fleeting, as elusive as spirit can be.

Spiritus in Latin is both "breath" and "life." The coinherence of meanings here doesn't *solve* any of the perplexities of the mind–body problem. But poetry does give one a literal pause in the moment, a momentary reconciliation of paradox that is the precursor of vision. It comes to me in the paradoxes of my pregnancy—a heightening of both sensation and thought—and challenges me to see how God is doing a new thing in these circumstances and for the sake of wholeness.

The intrusion of the physical certainly does arrest our attention, whether in pain, actual change, or loss of the ease or stamina we have taken for granted. It is not to be ignored or underrated—or spiritualized.

In *Illness as Metaphor*, Susan Sontag writes,

> In the plague-ridden England of the late sixteenth and seventeenth centuries . . . it was widely believed that "the happy man would not get plague." The fantasy that a happy state of mind would fend off disease probably flourished for all infectious diseases, before the nature of infection was understood. Theories that diseases are caused by mental states and can be cured by will power are always an index of how much is not understood about the physical terrain of a disease.

She adds that these theories, with their metaphorical applications, can be highly unfair to actual sufferers—sometimes producing guilt that inhibits healing.

I have also been reading how *important* mental attitudes and support of loved ones can be in conquering disease. The role of psychology in healing is a tricky one, and researchers are careful not to draw simplistic conclusions. Psychologist Martin E. P. Seligman, who has done studies showing relationships between individuals' explanations of why bad things happen and their rate of recovery, cautions: "If a crane falls on you, it doesn't matter what you think. If the magnitude of your cancer is overwhelming, your psychological outlook counts for zero. On the other hand, if your cancer is marginal or if an illness is just beginning, your psychological state may be critical."

The body and the mind do coinhere, but we do not always understand how one affects the other, and we are on safer ground if we admit to mystery and use our knowledge for healing rather than for judgment.

Pregnancy is certainly not a disease, but it also, among physical states, serves to clarify and challenge some assumptions about mind and body. For me, at this time, it brings into perspective what is most important in a given moment. My body does take precedence over my mind, especially since the "mind" could not function without it. Urgent needs of health, nutrition, or safety can stir even the domestic philosopher and armchair theologian from her contemplation to some immediate action.

This too is the grace of God. We were never meant to worship the mind. The physical keeps us in balance.

The prophet Isaiah sees God's preservation of the people

as a physical act—"I have taken you by the hand and kept you." Psalm 40:2 tells us that God has put our feet on a rock, making our steps secure. Our redemption is the most tangible of rescues—from whatever state of need; afterward comes the development of mind and spirit to do God's will.

This realization stirs my senses especially in Advent as we draw nearer to the celebration of God With Us. More understanding of the physical/spiritual nature of Messiah is being revealed to us through our own individual journeys as human beings, and in our corporate response that overflows toward one another in love. I feel our expectations and their fulfillment swelling as the weeks go by.

Someone is coming, and we anticipate knowing him, our Deliverer, in the very *isness* of our lives as humans. For me this means not only increased understanding, but action as well. I desire to give God more and more of myself; to become more attentive to what I should be about doing in my work and family and church life; to name Christ and declare him the source of the many blessings that enter my circle of awareness. I see the new thing that God is doing as part of the repair of creation—the curtain pulled back to reveal some of the glory of the design; the shared flashes of joy when relationships work and things jell. I see it when the balance for good outweighs evil for the moment; when someone moves toward belief; when an unexpected kindness changes my perspective. All these signs are indications of God's work in the world and in us, the pulling of the nets closer in to the center of God's will, as we edge gradually through these days toward the consummation of our hopes in Christ.

The movements of our wills toward the one Will, this is what it means to me this Advent to allow a new thing and welcome its wonders into my life.

When I am willing to be brought more and more into that wholeness, I enter a kind of prayer that was not possible before, in which I can say with the Psalmist:

> My heart is glad, and my soul rejoices;
>> my body also rests secure. (16:9)

Though we use the language of separation, distinguishing body from soul, yet in the prayer, in the synthesis of poetry, a wholeness of thought is possible in the moment. As we realize and live in our own wholeness, body and soul, we are all the more prepared to admit and to welcome Christ's incarnation, the coinhering of God and human flesh, glorious and healing—a new thing.

Lion and Lamb

The wolf shall live with the lamb,
the leopard shall lie down with the kid,
the calf and the lion and the fatling together,
and a little child shall lead them.

TONIGHT MY HUSBAND AND I were able to catch an hour or so together, to have dinner in a local restaurant before he had to leave for a meeting. Sitting across from each other in a booth helps us focus our communication, gives us space and time to catch up on what the other is doing and thinking.

He has been preaching a series of sermons on Advent themes. We have not really been comparing notes, yet it's surprising how our thoughts have moved in similar patterns over the Scripture passages we've been reading daily.

In preaching, he has the advantage of gauging the effect of his ideas and reflections in practically instant replay, observing the lively, spoken Word as it penetrates—and offends—its listeners. I must wait a considerably longer time for feedback from my writing, which is in every way a more solitary occupation.

How does one hear the Word and respond today? In

his sermons my husband has been trying to address this question, to prod his listeners into wondering what the Scripture means for their lives. It is another way of allowing people to discover how they themselves may enter the Advent story that is unfolding, so that they may become one with it. In talking about Mary and Joseph, for example, he does not try to explain or defend the virgin birth, but deals instead with the human dilemma of Joseph: his kindness not to put Mary away; his "yes" that became part of the preparation and conditions for Christ's birth to occur. Joseph's response to the lively Word was one of belief and action.

We talked about the Hebrew mind's receptivity to seeming contradiction. Biblical language is open; it does not require an either/or understanding in every case, but often allows for both/and. This inviting ambiguity provides room for our own entering into the scriptural event for a true encounter with the Word. Only in that way can it touch us in our peace of mind, our behavior, our choices, our understanding.

The ambiguity inherent in poetic language has rich implications for spirituality. Not only does it invite our response, it *requires* it in order for us to make meaning out of images—for instance, of the lion and lamb, or the camel going through the eye of the needle. Much of Old Testament wisdom literature is poetry. In writing of this literary form Gerhard von Rad says, "Basically the sense of a sentence was never completely fixed; any attempt to understand it was always a flexible one." It is sometimes tempting to forget that language is not as fixed as we might like it to be, and that even what we call "facts" are always open to interpretation. Owen Barfield, in his book *Poetic*

Diction, cautions us this way about the imprecision of language: "Meaning itself can never be conveyed from one person to another; words are not bottles; every individual must intuit meaning for himself, and the function of the poetic is to mediate such intuition by suitable suggestion."

Although Jesus' parables are not poetry, and the language of Paul is mainly exhortation, yet these ways of communicating, as well as the images and paradoxes they employed, were very much in line with the Hebrew tradition of "both/and"—a stretching of the poetic shoe to fit the foot that needed it. The rabbinic method of questions and answers, a dialectic that probes deeper not only into the subject, but into those taking part in the dialogue, adds a dimension of sharing the lively Word that can be lost if we lean only on lectures and authorities.

Paul wrote letters, inviting response. This view of "both/and" helps us to better understand some ambiguity he communicated about the end times. He could offer several scenarios, all that could give one pause and warning as well as offer comfort for those who had ears to hear.

Because Paul was a Jew, he saw everything in terms of creation and the handiwork of the Creator. In both language and style Paul took up the task of telling more of the story of God's dealing with Israel, in a reprise of the nation's history and choices. Gene M. Tucker says of that tradition, "Instead of generalizing about the nature or being of God, ancient Israel tended simply to tell the story of God's acts." To do that, the writers depended on images: fire and cloud, smoke on the mountain, Messiah as both Lion of Judah and Lamb of God.

We would not have the whole message without both the events of Israel and the images that embody God's work and nature. In *The Glass of Vision* Austin Farrer points out the importance of both events and images in the life of Christ. Images "set forth the supernatural mystery which is the heart of the teaching." Events without images, he says, "would be no revelation at all, and the images without the events would remain shadows on the clouds." Both are necessary, as one helps interpret the other; then the roles switch, in a kind of dance.

The season of Advent is surely wrapped in both image and event. The birth of a child to Mary and Joseph is an interesting story. But the images, the mystery, the promises, the human responses . . . all are necessary for us to make sense of it and enter it.

"Ambiguity" is not a very appealing word in a culture that equates "facts" with truth. Yet ambiguity has its place. Mystery invites us to enter, asking questions, placing demands on us, and engaging us in the process of revelation. In Scripture, centuries of ambiguity and poetry come to rest in a fact—a birth, the particularity in face and form of a boy child, arriving on a specific day in the fullness of time, son of a maiden, protected by an earthly father. At the incarnation, the event of God With Us, the images are concrete, at one with the birth.

Lion of Judah, Lamb of God, mighty God, everlasting Father, Prince of Peace: The glorious images converge in the sprout of a historical family tree:

> A shoot shall come out from the stump of Jesse,
> > and a branch shall grow out of his roots. (Isa. 11:1)

Jesus could not be more securely rooted in the family of Israel than this. King David's father is singled out here, from among the patriarchs, rather than David himself, who would have served to make a symbolic point about kingship. Yet it is Jesse, father of the young shepherd, the less legendary man, whose other sons were found unsuited. Only lastly was David chosen and appointed, the least likely to serve, a king of humble origin like that of the One he foreshadowed.

Dealing with both the images and the events this Advent is important to us as we try to share the gospel in different ways. Is this yet another dimension of the body–mind problem, the reconciling of head and heart, vocation and desire, as we share our own lives and let them mingle with the message? In our parish and beyond we see increasingly how physical life and the experiences of individuals are taken up and become one with the message itself, as those individuals consent to it. The events occur first and are never *less* than the meaning that can be made of them—in fact, the interpretation itself is dependent on the physical events. But the images shine through the events and bring them into focus—on Christ, the One who has come, is coming, and will come.

His coming is that Event toward which Advent is striving with its images, even in the paradox of the lion and lamb. In the expectation of his coming we are able to gather up these images, shadows of forthtelling, glimpses as in a mirror, and take further steps into the heart of the mystery.

We leave the restaurant. I return to the house to do my work and finish wrapping the last of the Christmas presents.

We are holding onto meaning. There is a sense of movement in our own history—a rootedness in this time, this place. The awareness of this holds us in belief as we perform our own distinct tasks. Without this shared meaning our lives would be fragmented, more closely mirroring our broken age. So we take care to support each other's callings with prayer that penetrates these hours of separation. We look for the wholeness that can accommodate the tension of many things going on, images of truth that flash and then disappear, events that cannot yet be interpreted in the flux of time. It is the same faith in the redemptiveness of daily life that holds us in theological belief.

We cannot imagine how the lion and the lamb may be reconciled: in our selves, our parish, the world's denouement. But we have cast our lot here, in the midst of the ongoing story, for better or worse.

The City

Your life and your death are with your neighbour.

*T*HE EVENTS AND IMAGES of Advent are converging more and more as the days progress toward Christmas. As I have been reading Scripture passages designated for Advent, many images present themselves, and today I encounter a glorious one concerned mainly with the third level of Advent: the coming future.

I find this image in the Book of Revelation's description of a new heaven and a new earth: Jerusalem, the Holy City, coming down out of heaven from God, prepared as a bride adorned for her husband. St. John's voice proclaims the familiar mystery of the incarnation, but in cosmic terms: "See, the home of God is among mortals. . . ." God will dwell with them as their God, and they will be God's people. This is the consummation of our Advent hope.

I have been concerned with personal things this Advent, the inner growth and preparation of my own heart. But *the city* is an image that takes up and includes my inner world. The community of believers, of which I am a part, and the community of work, to which I also relate, are components of the city. This broader network serves to keep us aware of more than ourselves.

The city of God is yet to come in its fullness, but in another sense it surrounds us already; many hearts are being prepared, and in different ways acknowledging that *the dwelling of God is with God's people.* This is the purpose of icons, and it underlies any corporate celebration of praise. The image of the city reminds me of the vastness of God's work of grace, as reflected in Beatrice's words to Dante in Paradise: "Behold our city; how wide it spreads its gyres."

Charles Williams, who wrote extensively of the city as an image of hope, lived in London and worked as an editor and proofreader for Oxford University Press. He loved cities, finding even in the bleaker aspects of urban landscapes some signs of order and design. In Williams's novel *All Hallows' Eve,* a character expresses delight in even the grimier features of the city:

> The Thames was dirty and messy. Twigs, bits of
> paper and wood, cords, old boxes drifted on it.
> Yet . . . it was not a depressing sight. The dirtiness
> of the water was, at that particular point, what
> it should be, and therefore pleasant enough. The
> evacuations of the City had their place in the City;
> how else could the City be the City? . . . These
> things also were facts.

Humphrey Carpenter writes of Williams, in *The Inklings,*

> To Charles Williams the City, with its churches,
> its law courts, its business houses, banks, libraries

and printing presses, seemed the expression of an ideal order. The City's rigid hierarchies and rules, as well as its love of pageantry and ritual, delighted his imagination and seemed to him refreshingly stable and unshakable after the uncertainties and worries of his parents' home. Indeed to him the City of London soon became an earthly expression of the ultimate City, the City of God.

In this Williams acknowledged his debt to Augustine's *The City of God*. Yet rather than seeing two totally separate cities—heavenly and earthly—as Augustine did, Williams emphasized how the two coinhered, interpenetrated at every point. It was always possible to step across any ordinary threshold and find oneself in the throes of a life or death choice, in the precincts of heaven or hell. This understanding of the city is necessary to Williams's view of the incarnation and its effect on all of human life, here and now as well as in the future.

But it is not surprising that today, no less than in Augustine's time, the image of the city seems almost ludicrous as any kind of ideal. Now the city may remind us of urban decay and blight, rioting and poverty, hunger and homelessness, crime and perversion in the streets. The city has been compared to a living organism of interdependent cells, which now suffers from disease. What is meant to promote cooperation and healthy functioning has become another image of chaos.

Madison Smartt Bell ably uses the image of the city in his novel *Waiting for the End of the World*: a character encounters "the enchanted city, which he well knew to be unreachable. More elusive than a simple mirage, it did not

only recede before him but hid behind him and on either side, whenever he tried to enter it." In this fascinat-
ing story of New York City low life, the image still holds
strong in mocking the reality of its modern state. In the
same novel, a young child, born to privilege, is fooled by
the illusion of the city, and seeing its lights fanning out to
the limits of the horizon, "assumed that the chains of light
were baubles already his own."

Despite areas of ruin and decay, even today the city
lures, compels, stirs the imagination. And there are indications that the city—here and in future realization—can
only be entered into by grace.

I worked once with an artist, Hugh Claycombe, who
created in pen and ink his rendering of the City—the
Bride—composed of multitudes of vague figures, faces, am-
biguous shapes streaming in concert to meet the Bridegroom. And the composite shape (when viewed as a whole,
without the distraction of detail) formed an overall female
shape, a Bride. The whole effect conveyed a beauty and
dignity that a simple line drawing from one perspective
could never achieve—as the problem of the one and the
many seemed momentarily resolved through his art.

It offered a flash, a glimpse of what "may be"—as do
the lines of poetry in Revelation, or the picture I have over
my desk of Dante and Beatrice with the divine souls in
Paradise, who appear above as points of light, reflections
of the glory of their Creator.

Charles Williams writes: "There is no final idea for
us but the glory of God in the redeemed and universal
union—call it Man or the Church or the City." He saw the
opposite of this great image as "the Infamy"—the old root

of chaos, the tentacled monster of me-ism. "There is, in the end," he wrote, "no compromise between the two; there is only choice." Thus the unity that is redeemed mankind, the City, is held together by will, unlike a nation or race, which exists by birthright or chance.

I see in this the echoing of the ancient theme of the Two Ways from Deuteronomy 30:19: "I have set before you life and death, blessings and curses. Choose life so that you and your descendants may live." Moses challenged the people of Israel in those early days to choose the Way of Life and thus propel themselves on a course toward the City, long before Jerusalem was a reality or even an image.

We can imagine the kinds of dilemmas that the people of Israel faced in choosing life or death. Idolatry was only one of many temptations; the Ten Commandments covered that and most of the others. These people were dealing with the same human nature we struggle with today. This realization challenges us also to be about building the City by our daily actions toward others. We are to trim back the hedges that separate, restrain the chaos monster, choose civilization, and practice courtesy and respect toward all souls. All our choices for life do matter, and help deflect the Infamy—the lie that we ourselves are the center—and the anarchy that follows.

For Williams, as for all the saints, the belief in blessing every creature is seen as essential to the spiritual life. He points out that "definition" of differences among the City's occupants is unavoidable, but such definition (or description) is intended to help order the City's life in one particular way or another. Differences among us point out the need for "traffic regulations" for the convenience of patterns of movement among people. That is what laws and rules serve to do—to make civility the norm. But they cannot teach us to love one another.

The Infamy seeks to lead people to exclude others on the basis of difference, to enslave or annihilate. Williams calls us as Christians to "a courtesy of carriage towards facts other than ourselves, a recognition of the creation even when that creation appears to us displeasing."

The challenge begins and ends with the doctrine of creation—whether to admit the coinherence of all life of which we are a part, or to separate ourselves and deny *what is* when it does not suit us. Williams reminds us that the Glory is always for us to observe and acknowledge in others. Agreeing to a healthy exchange of life in the City means very literally bearing one another's burdens, he writes, quoting both St. Anthony ("Your life and your death are with your neighbour") and William Law ("I am to love myself as I love my neighbour or any other created being, that is, only in and for God").

If I ever have any glimpse of the City, of the unity that is part of Christ's coming, it is in the Eucharist. There both familiar and new people, collected for that day, meet in thanksgiving and exchange of gifts at the altar. I have noticed over a period of time that the repeated experience of taking communion with the same people can bring a transfiguration of common faces, temporarily overshadowing divisions and weaknesses. The open palms to receive Christ at best imply a unity of will and purpose. As we leave the Lord's table I am sometimes struck at the awesome task of bearing in our bodies something of Christ to each other. I believe our fellowship and commonality tangibly unite us, and that any who come in belief can mesh with the purposes of divine love that sustain the City.

Somehow differences are less relevant in the light of the mutual exchanges in the Body. Through gifts of thanksgiving and service, we constantly experience a reordering of the levels of need and fulfillment, part of the "Great Dance," a pattern of the City.

This experience of the transfiguration of human flesh substantiates what we know of God's purposes for souls—that God will not eradicate our individuality. The City is not an amalgam of faceless and undifferentiated beings. Rather as we take the journey from here to there, through the Eucharist and other rites of courtesy and exchange, we travel expecting that we will recognize ourselves and each other when we arrive at our destination.

Dew in April

May he be like rain that falls on the mown grass,
like showers that water the earth.

C HICAGO HAS HAD RECORD cold temperatures now
for three days in a row, on top of more than six inches
of snow. We have been through winters like this before. In
the midst of such a siege the cold becomes an entity in
itself, invading one's consciousness and causing us to order
our lives in different ways. We make our choices as to what
we will accomplish—both errands and visits—on the basis
of the stress and added complexity of battling winter.

The cold is only one hardship in our otherwise quite
comfortable lives. When I am inside and protected it
makes my present security seem even richer. Having to
face it from time to time gives me some insight into the
harshness of Advents past. In earlier times when the conditions for human life in winter were cruel, those hard-
ships inspired some of the loveliest carols that portray the
softness and subtlety of Christ's birth, in contrast to the
rigors of the winter season.

One of these I listen to often in Advent is a lovely,
artful medieval folk lyric, "I Sing of a Maiden," which re-

minds us that Jesus' conception took place in another, gentler season. It is described delicately as:

> He came all so stille
>> Where his mother lay,
> As dew in Aprille
>> That falleth on the spray.

This reminds me of a line from a psalm I have recently read in my devotions, which may even be a source of the carol's lines. "May he be like rain that falls on the mown grass, like showers that water the earth" (Ps. 72:6). It is part of a prayer for King Solomon, but the metaphor is so beautifully applicable to the coming of another king. Our human desire for his light touch, his all-pervading presence, is another aspect of Jesus' coming. To each of us he can fall as dew, softening an otherwise harsh existence. Especially to those who suffer in this season, this is a welcome strain. His coming is not to be only in fire and smoke and thunder. For, "how silently," how inwardly, "the wond'rous gift is giv'n" in hearts that have prepared for him to come, as dew in April that settles on the grass.

I love the simplicity of the image in this carol, which suggests Christ's conception in earthly time—in spring, a definite spot on the calendar. It is a word of promise that will be fulfilled in actual birth.

The human and the divine, the unexpected and the ordinary, meet in this small scene. Even pilgrims struggling in the throes of winter and its accompanying ills could celebrate God's touch, the wonder of incarnation as it became part of the human story.

Another small picture of the delicacy of Christ's coming is sketched in one of my favorite carols. Based upon an image of Mary, it is the third in Benjamin Britten's *A Ceremony of Carols*:

There is no rose of such vertu
As is the rose that bare Jesu.
Alleluia.

For in this rose conteinèd was
Heaven and earth in litel space,
Res miranda [A wonderful thing].

By that rose we may well see
There be one God in persons three,
Pares forma [Of like form]. . . .

Leave we all this werldly mirth,
And follow we this joyful birth.
Transeamus [Let us pass over from this world to
the other].

This exquisite carol with its Latin responses—a way of teaching theology through beauty—is to me a complete but miniature image, like a tiny crèche resting in a nutshell. It is all there: the juxtaposition of heaven and earth "in litel space," the affirmation of the Trinity behind the miracle; and there is even room for our response of action and procession from here to God's kingdom.

The traditional medieval carol has its boisterous as well as its sober side, as carols are a direct descendant of the vocally accompanied "round dance" in which a leader would carry the stanza and the participants respond in the "burden," or refrain. These carols are a striking example of how the church transformed an essentially secular musical form into a popular Christian litany. Carols are true "folk" religion, and meet the participant in his or her condition. In a season of harshness they bring hidden hope, a note of joy and even of frivolity creeping into the tone.

In order to teach in this common language of music and participation, some carol writers borrowed meter and even quoted from the earliest Latin hymns. And although the singers probably did not know Latin, the lines of Christian admonition were familiar and conveyed the "religious" point to them. Richard Leighton Greene points out, "The distinctive charm of many carols is just that they do belong to two worlds; they were written in days when one could be pious and merry at the same time."

The carols help us to see how it was possible to live in harsh conditions of poverty and disease, with short life spans and much deprivation, while continuing to savor the small human joys that are part of our lot, and even sing and dance for their duration. Somehow this attitude has a Christian ring to it that we may miss amid our comfort and plenty. The carols of the medieval age are a reminder that hardship does not necessarily weaken one's openness to God or lessen the ability to recognize and enjoy God's small mercies. The real cost of daily life is never foreign to our taste for God, but rather the condition under which we are *most* likely to seek God—to experience God as both immanent and transcendent—a paradox that was never easy, and is perhaps even harder for modern minds.

These paradoxes, like the expectation of Christ's coming future, are jarring to our senses unless we refresh ourselves with the sweep of the story of our salvation and experience the gentleness of his coming. Our awareness of Advent is meant to be apocalyptic—expectant as well as celebrative. The dew in April, the Rose of birth, the cradle and cross are meaningful to us only as we consider an ongoing story that is moving somewhere, gathering up the events as well as the images toward a consummation yet to be.

This week I have been reading manuscripts of several apocalyptic novels that were submitted to the publisher I work for. They are stories that try to capture in narrative detail the place and the hour of Christ's second coming to earth.

There is something wrong with all of them, but it is hard to put my finger (or editing pencil) on. Madison Smartt Bell says in his fine novel *Waiting for the End of the World* that "Doomsday in the abstract had limited audience appeal." Doomsday has to be enfleshed, like the first coming in all its particularity, to touch us at all. These authors have attempted to set up scenarios into which the end might come, in cataclysm and upheaval; yet it is the lack of believable reality in the lives of the characters as they bring the authors' theology into play that disappoints me every time. I look for the juxtaposition of the ordinary and the unexpected to be rendered more skillfully. These novelists haven't given us the full-blown humanity, the rootedness in daily life and believable situation, that is necessary for us to identify with characters and say, "Yes, that is how it is"—or how it could be. Rather than investing in the development of character, the writers seem to indulge themselves in intricate plotting, clever coincidence of events that might signal the end of all things. Some attempts fail worse than others.

Carefulness of theology (echoing verse and chapter of Revelation) is not enough in this kind of writing. Authors may succeed on the side of affirming God's sovereignty and power, but fail in incarnational terms to show *how God comes to us* in subtlety and gentleness. Something in me expects that Coming Future also to be all-pervading as the soft rain that waters the earth.

Perhaps we are always a bit uncomfortable with the awesome reality of incarnation itself, of Christ's conception and all of the subsequent intermingling of human and divine that follows in the story. Taking Christ's humanity seriously and concluding what it then requires of us is painful and demanding.

I read many writers' attempts to affirm a theology of the Last Judgment, but find few examples of writing that truly allow God to appear or accurately portray a humanity open to redemption. Without that incarnational dimension, theology comes off, at best, as irrelevant.

In novels, at least, it seems that characters have to breathe first, be incarnations of some reality in the author's own soul, and bear a ring of truth about them. They cannot be mere figures on a plotted chess board, programmed on a propagandistic mission.

The novels that have most involved me in the scandal and glory of incarnation are not necessarily apocalyptic: François Mauriac's *Vipers' Tangle* comes to mind; Frederick Buechner's *Godric*; Charles Williams's novels, especially *All Hallows' Eve*; Olov Hartman's *Holy Masquerade.* In these novels I find a combination of the subtlety of God's coming and the overwhelming power of a realization that is life-changing. Movement toward belief, it seems, whether in life or its artful imitation, is always particular, always individual. To be able to capture the tracings of that movement is almost as tricky as bottling the dew of an April morning, and the heavy-handedness of many writers simply blows away the evidence.

Our lives do not read like a novel—they simply go on day by day. Some days we think we can make sense of some of the strains of movement, but we always lack the omniscience of one who views it all from every perspective. Novelists assume an almost God-like stance to do their work as creators. They make meaning out of particulars, and give it all a beginning and middle and end. I do not have such clear lines to work with in making sense of these days, of interpreting the instances of incarnation around and within me. But as I am nearing the close of this season and drawing some conclusions as to what has happened, I am aware that I have grown, so that my humanity makes contact with the divine at more points. The plot thickens. Jesus' coming, his *comings* in silence and in power, are more of a reality to me than when I began.

Escalating Grace

All the death that ever was, set next to life, would scarcely fill a cup.

L AST NIGHT ON THE EVENING NEWS, suffering people in freezing apartments were being inter-viewed by reporters wearing ski jackets. These were ten-ants who hadn't paid their utility bills and were living without heat. Some had already survived the coldest weeks on record for the month of December in Chicago, which is saying quite a bit. The cruel incongruity is that these people are being interviewed and so providing news sto-ries for commercial television, but are not being helped on the spot through this publicity. Perhaps that will follow, and human kindness will yet win out.

This could almost be a scenario of the last days. In the midst of this bitter cold spell, tribulation has fallen upon some already, through no fault of their own.

The cold hurts flesh; it stings. How, in a civilized city, a sophisticated culture, can this deprivation be allowed to exist? At least eighty people have died so far, from the ad-versary Winter. What does this apocalyptic season have to say of those losses in a time intended for expectation and hope, not death?

This evening we had an early celebration with some parishioners. It was a bountiful turkey dinner with all the special touches, and we prayed, "Lord, make us ever mindful of the needs of others." As an image of the earlier newscast flashed through my mind, it was not pleasant to be reminded of it in the midst of our ease, and of the luxuries on which we depend to cheer and sustain us. I didn't want to think about those people without heat, but I couldn't get them out of my mind. Those of us who have given our usual donations and answered some individual needs as they've been presented to us could easily say, "We gave at the office." Why, we wonder, did these people have no backup plan for such an emergency—to stay with relatives or borrow money for bills? But all ropes have an end, and these people had reached theirs. Are our own ropes shorter than we'd like to believe?

How do we talk of the City and of the glory, of the hope of Christ's coming in the face of real deprivation and particular life-threatening situations? All my thoughts seem to be coming out as questions. At this stage of my reflections on the beauty and lessons of this season, it seems I am right back at square one with the necessity for faith, belief that it all means what we declare it to mean: rest for the weary, release for the captives, eternal fulfillment in that holy city which has "no need of sun or moon . . . for the glory of God is its light, and its lamp is the Lamb." We read that its gates will never be shut, nor shall there be any night (Rev. 21:23, 25).

If I correctly understand the nature of apocalyptic literature, it is addressed to those who still live in the realm of human choice about the "way of life" and the "way of death": citizens on earth who are allowed a peek, a glimpse of what might be, as an admonition to choose life. The message here is not just warning us that only those who choose life will see this city. For apocalyptic writing is also a literature of *attraction*, reflecting a hope so glorious it is meant to *compel* seekers into belief, into participation in the glory that is to come.

To me it is a reminder that it is not enough simply to meet human needs here on earth; it is urgent that we direct people to the Source of all gifts and all healing in Christ. Neither is it enough to drum a message of salvation and future relief from suffering into people who cannot respond until their immediate needs are met. But to me this vision in Revelation contains hints of both—physical comfort and peace, and eternal rest in the kingdom of the Lamb.

No cold, no closed doors, no turned-off heat, no more deprivation. God's rescue of souls is a tangible and physical redemption. In God's love, all needs are to be met so that we may share in this eternal kingdom. How can the church begin to offer both solutions to immediate needs and the hope of Christ which it carries into the world through its very existence? How do we embody its message of rest for the weary, release for the captives? It is not enough simply to point others to Scripture if we ourselves are not willing to be part of the answer, becoming one with the scenario of redemption, healing and restoring in the name and power of Christ.

Images of suffering on TV have some effect on me; but real encounter with individual need always has so much more impact. Not long ago I heard that an elderly friend and church helper was being evicted from his apartment because he couldn't afford the extra rent hike, and I was able to find him some financial help through my husband's discretionary fund. Praying with him through that crisis was not a mental effort—it was like breathing; it came naturally because of the particularity of the pain on that face, the reality of my investment in the friendship, and the threat of the cold streets, of possible loss of belongings and way of life. What I had to give monetarily was very limited, as we are not rich. This is where the church becomes a buffer to keep out the cold, hold back the onslaught, until the real day of the City, the light and heat of the kingdom, can reach all the faithful who have been left out in this world.

Though it is easier to care about those we know personally who are in need, to express our empathy, our true identification with their suffering surely is limited. To go any deeper into others' pain involves trust in an all-knowing, all-caring God, and in the principle I like to call "escalating grace." I see this as the kind of rescue that meets each seeker in the exact moment and condition of need, and is always as powerful as is necessary, in God's economy, to fill in whatever gap, make bearable whatever suffering. We may need only quick relief in some states of distress, or an assurance that "a check is in the mail." And this, too, is grace. But as the agonies of life thicken and multiply, so I believe (from what times I've experienced it) that escalating grace is available, and comes swiftly and completely at any level.

I have long wondered whether martyrs become transfigured in their pain, glorified and purged in one and the same instant from the awful reality of suffering and death. We do not know the mercy that may prevail even in such a death, in untimely death, or the purity of penultimate agony. No one who has experienced it has ever returned to tell of it.

We do not want such horrific knowledge, if it can only be got firsthand. I believe that somewhere between real pain and real glory is the truth—that death has no sting in the end, the grave no victory. Only in such language do we dare (I tremble at attempting) to speak of such things.

I believe God is with us, in hearts who welcome the coming at any point—in the moment of greatest need, even in death. I strain to express a hope in the reality of escalating grace, that finds not even death on a cross to be foreign domain.

I do know that how we live here matters; and how we die matters. "Lord, save us from dying suddenly and unpreparèd," we pray in the Great Litany. It is a wise prayer. The only way to live is to walk prepared for death, as for the coming. Miles Coverdale, in his *Fruitful Lessons Upon the Passion*, writes:

> Death is [loathsome] and very terrible unto the flesh;
> but joyful and welcome it is unto all such as are
>   instructed
> in the secret science of God.

Precious in the sight of the Lord is the death of God's saints.

The Christian gospel—and those who bear it—are never very many steps from death, in their message, in their risks, in the stakes they represent. Any talk of ultimate life carries with it the awareness of death and its consequences. It is built into the structure of grace.

The more we are able gradually to face death—our own, others' we love—the less, I believe, we have to fear. I am convinced that there are graces yet unknown to us, because they are not yet needed; and God is, we believe, economical. Grace is never an excuse for us to do nothing in the face of others' needs; it is merely our own last hope and "cushion" as humans, when we have fought to the nth for survival and clearly must turn toward the other door.

Escalating grace is, in fact, so compelling and overriding that we can only hope and pray to be at times God's instruments in its workings. Grace is a widening stream that washes over us, far excelling our own actions toward God, but covering and including as a sacrifice all that is offered.

I find something of this notion of escalating grace magnificently reflected in Frederick Buechner's novel *Godric*. It is a fictional narrative of the historical Anglo-Saxon monk of that name, based on the sketchy record available of his life. By entering Godric's thoughts as he tells his story to his biographer and fellow monk, Reginald, Buechner presents the reader with the flesh and bones of a believable life, and depicts the relentless struggle of a truly human saint.

After Godric spent half a life in squandering and using others shamelessly, seeking pleasure and personal gain, God touched him. A heart "took root" and began to grow in him. He eventually sold all his goods, left home, and began the life of a hermit at Finchale, on the River Wear near Durham, England.

In a moment of vision, looking back on his life, he reflects:

> What's lost is nothing to what's found, and all the death that ever was, set next to life, would scarcely fill a cup.

Grace is what *does* fill each cup, each person alone knowing within his or her own story how that is so. This is the vision that connects God's saints, though they are separated by time or bodily presence. Godric's assurance reflects the peace that "passes understanding."

We have the testimony of the saints and the assurances of Scripture. It is in the hope of escalating grace that we approach the end of this Advent.

A Quiet Habitation

. . . a quiet habitation, an immovable tent,
whose stakes will never be pulled up . . .

LAST NIGHT WE HAD A pre-Christmas celebration with my parents, knowing it would be the last holiday in that house. They have sold it and will be moving to a smaller one when my father retires in April.

It was bitter cold on the hour's trip to their home in the suburbs, and our car windows never did totally clear, giving us low visibility as well as a never-quite-warm interior. We were thankful as we pulled into their driveway and saw the lights on, and my father quickly opening the door to speed us inside.

The house had been decorated sparsely, since there are no young children around to impress. It was just the four of us this year. My parents' current foster daughter—they have helped raise more than ten foster children since I left home—was spending the holiday with her birth mother. My mother had sent the family food and presents; last year their Christmas meal had been potatoes and macaroni, we later found out.

My parents are constantly giving things away, and their

plans to move to a smaller house have only accelerated their giving. They have always held things lightly, happier with sharing them and spreading love through gifts than keeping it all for themselves. They load up our car (sometimes to barely closing) each time we visit them. Last night they included a little rocking chair along with the presents—they are already getting excited about their first grandchild.

Once again, in my thoughts, I am narrowing down. This home and family have held and sheltered me. This particular abode has been for me a microcosm of the City itself, a corner of the kingdom—from the early days when my parents first taught me of Jesus. No cosmic image carries much weight without the actual events of a common life, the jarring particularity of home and hearth, specific faces around the fire or table, foibles and differences, struggles to break free and hold on, sometimes both at once. This is family; home is here, and through my own connectedness to these people I know something of the web of workings of the human family, and occasionally glimpse my own progress toward the City in manageable perspective.

Tonight our thoughts are simple and centered. As a family we join together to read the gospel narrative and say prayers for the opening of our hearts to Christ's imminent coming. We prepare to welcome a feast in the midst of this coldness, to lighten our hearts and spirits, and also to fill them. They have grown to know more of him and his comings, through these years and weeks of seeking him.

We wait expectantly, as the words of Isaiah promise: "Your eyes will see the king in his beauty" (Isa. 33:17). It is fitting that a city have a king; the Lord and his land are part of our hope, since we expect to dwell with him.

> Look on Zion, the city of our appointed festivals!
>   Your eyes will see Jerusalem,
>   a quiet habitation, an immovable tent,
>   whose stakes will never be pulled up,
>   and none of whose ropes will be broken. (v. 20)

This verse describes a humbler habitation, a much less glorious vision of permanence than the City in Revelation with its walls and gates and precious stones (21:12–27). A house along the way is more like the habitations we ourselves dwell in. This passage was a fitting promise of continuity to a wayfaring people in the desert, who had to travel light. Today as we narrow down and let go of things we thought we needed, we show that what we truly value is our relationship to our Lord, who will make us "at home" wherever he is. Our possessions do not sustain us, and too often they entangle us needlessly. Our very pilgrimage is a lesson in how to live off the gifts of life that are given day to day.

Yet how we long, even now, for a continuing city, a permanent habitation. Our imagination grows, it seems, with our days spent here. As we mature we find it takes more to satisfy that desire, our longing for settledness and security.

I am thankful for the stability of the home my parents have given me for so many years, a "quiet habitation" that has been a refuge also for others. They have given an address and a home to so many children, helping their young imaginations grow toward a belief in permanence, something most have never before had the luxury of knowing. How can displaced children know what a family is and how it works unless they have lived in one? My parents have

kept many children from having to live in institutions—
or worse. They have opened themselves to be hurt many
times, in hopes of helping these children—only to be un-
appreciated and turned on by already-scarred young teen-
agers. But they have kept at it, and haven't stopped giving
away what they have to give.

How sheltered I was in early life, knowing home to
be the circle of their love, in a household that prayed and
honored God. My imagination was fostered by this secure
abode, and allowed to soar—and return—to a protected
center. No home or family is perfect, but the gift of understood permanence has to be one of my childhood's greatest legacies.

It takes some notion of permanence, some taste of stability in a relationship to stretch our capacity to rest in another
person—to form an adult bonding on a solid basis. We
all seek "a local habitation, and a name," to borrow Shake-
speare's phrase. Such a longing for home and security is a
whetting of our appetites for the City. Our lessons in the
family surely are part of our preparation here—for learning
the meaning of community and mutuality and unity of will.
The people, the Lord, the City—all are connected.

From the comfort of my habitation I am reminded
that Jesus himself had not a place to lay his head. He had
only the manger, which he hallowed by his presence—as
we sometimes make our homes and resting places of more
significance by the dignity of thanksgiving. What power
we have as humans, in how we treat our own abodes and
how we prepare our hearts, which are also Christ's abode.

This is what his coming is about—his dwelling among
us. And tonight we are planning and preparing for tomorrow night's Christmas Eve service. How are we, on a cold,

inhospitable night, to stretch others' understanding of permanence? What part of the kingdom are we? We are a small parish, part of the web of the whole. As a microcosm of the City, composed of many families, we represent various ages and styles of servanthood. Some are descendants of families who have worshiped within these stone walls in decades past.

Our church is a habitation, a shelter; sometimes it is a place of quiet and contemplation. In it we enact mysteries that none of us could explain or exhaust in a million lifetimes. We enter in, as pilgrims do, on the way to and from our homes. Our Lord goes with us, and our love and concerns reach out, touching others' lives. Each year that passes we become more deeply rooted in this way of life.

The church and my own home have been shelters, quiet habitations that have allowed me to take this journey inward and outward this Advent. I sit now at a typewriter, a most modern tool, while engaged in an ancient quest, *to know.* I seek to make some sense of my paces in this particular season. I must offer this work as a sacrifice of thanksgiving, an offering of peace from my own life and vocation.

Though there have been flashes of insight for me, images that stir my vision and hopes, I realize that this is only a cutaway segment of a lifelong pilgrimage. Welcoming all the wonders of Advent has provided me with places to rest momentarily as I continue the journey.

For me, the writing and praying have overlapped in one intent, to praise and to seek to "come down where I ought to be." But just now my prayer is specifically for others: for all who will hear the Word. For my husband, for his strength and stamina; he has been up late nights preparing sermons for Christmas Eve, Christmas Day, St. Stephen,

St. John, Holy Innocents. For our child, who will enter a world such as this.

The church calendar is a reminder that we are not only at an end, but at a beginning as well. We come now to a point of centering—on a feast. This is where we are to be at this point in the flow of days. The exactness of the date saves us from any doubt. Christmas Eve is only hours away.

Home is here; love is here; Christ is here.

What Child Is This?

Arise, thou Sun so longed for. . . .

*I*T IS CHRISTMAS EVE and the paradox stands. We have been held for the last four weeks of Advent in the tension between expectation and realization, and now this tautness turns to release. Self-examination melts into praise; waiting basks in fulfillment; hope turns to joy.

Christ's coming is both a cosmic revealing and a hidden thing . . . God is known to us in paradox: in flesh and in spirit.

I have a sense that my preparation and expectation will be mirrored in another day of birth I will experience in a few months. I look forward to the celebration that will then break the tension of waiting for my own child.

This is what it has all been about from the very beginning: a Child, born into the rush of time, redeeming time and those who dwell in its confines.

This, this is Christ the king
  Whom shepherds guard and angels sing.
Haste, haste to bring him laud—
  The babe, the son of Mary.

We have come once again to behold him in the sanctuary, in our own neighborhood parish church. The fine carved wooden angels on either side of the altar stand as always, playing their instruments in his honor.

Our Christmas Eve celebration this year involves old and new elements; new and old faces; cherished traditions with slight variations. The Christ candle now beams in the center of our Advent wreath. After weeks of the absence of flowers, many poinsettia pots flank the altar in bright thanksgiving. The red bows are a sign of hope against the dark interior walls.

The ordered sequence of the weeks has brought us to the bedside of this babe, to the declaration that this child is indeed Christ the Lord, the One toward whom all our waiting and expectation have been directed. And it is not in vain.

> For he will come like a rushing stream,
>   which the wind of the LORD drives.

> "And he will come to Zion as Redeemer,
>   to those in Jacob who turn from transgression,
>   says the LORD." (Isa. 59:19–20, RSV)

Seventy-five people have braved the cold to come and gather as a church family, first for Lessons and Carols, and then for the Eucharist. Some couldn't come—it was so cold by 10:00 PM that their cars wouldn't start. Others of our parish were out of town; some who said they would be here are not. It is a small enough church to notice presence and absence. But the celebration goes on, the beginning of the feast of Christmastide, which will go on for twelve more days. Its breadth simply cannot be confined to one night or day's work of praise.

We come to speak the name of Jesus, to confess him as Lord in this place, in the light of this season, the darkness of this hour. If one more person confesses him along with us this year, that is a marked progression toward the kingdom. Isaiah spoke of the importance of God's covenant with us that is intended to last "from this time forth and for evermore."

Christmas is here for another year, and the calendar leads us toward Epiphany, that season of the further revealing of Christ, his purposes for us and for the world.

After the service, we shared the news of our expected child with the congregation, and we received many warm congratulations and hugs. Now that we are telling people openly, it is a kind of relief. Already we have had promises of a crib, a bassinet, and other baby furniture. Plans are forming to redecorate the study as a nursery.

Our lives are one with the lives of these people, fellow believers for whom Christ came, is coming, and will come. Seeing their familiar faces and sharing in both joy and praise with them gives us strength to envision other people who will join us in future years. It encourages hopes for greater complexity and unity within the Body of Christ in times to come. Thus our prayers expand to touch God's larger purposes in the world, beyond our own walls and streets.

> Arise, thou Sun so longed for . . .
> We plead, O Lord, to see
> The day of earth's redemption,
> And ever be with thee!

Sources

Advent One

SUNDAY

Romans 13:11b–12a.

George Herbert, *The Country Parson.*

Coventry Patmore, *The Rod, the Root, and the Flower.*

Psalm 16:6.

MONDAY

1 Corinthians 15:46.

"Father, we thank thee . . . ," *Didache* (trans. F. Bland Tucker).

Luci Shaw, "A Celibate Epiphany," *The Sighting* (Wheaton, IL, 1981), used by permission.

TUESDAY

Richard Crashaw, "Hymn in the Holy Nativity."

WEDNESDAY

Carroll E. Simcox, "The Baal Shem, My Inscrutable Neighbor and I," *The Christian Century,* March 12, 1986.

William Griffin, *Clive Staples Lewis: A Dramatic Life* (San Francisco, 1986).

Charles Williams, *The Figure of Beatrice: A Study in Dante* (London, 1943).

Barbara Reynolds, *Introduction to Dante's Paradise,* Penguin Classics, 1962.

C. S. Lewis, *The Weight of Glory* (New York, 1981).

THURSDAY

Emily Dickinson, "Tell all the Truth but tell it slant –"

Collect for Advent III, *Book of Common Prayer.*

FRIDAY

Syrian Liturgy of St. James.

Athanasian Creed.

John 1:14.

SATURDAY

Robert Southwell, "This Little Babe."

"The Infant King," Basque carol.

Robert Southwell, "In Freezing Winter Night."

Advent Two

SUNDAY

Psalms 148, 149, 150.

"All lies in a passion of patience—my lord's rule," Charles Williams, *Taliessin Through Logres* (London, 1941).

MONDAY

Collect for Advent II, Book of Common Prayer.

TUESDAY

2 Peter 1: 3–4.

1 Thessalonians 5:13–14.

WEDNESDAY

Psalm 27:14.

Madeleine L'Engle, *A Circle of Quiet* (New York, 1972).

THURSDAY

Psalm 37:4.

Gerard Manley Hopkins, "Inscape."

FRIDAY

Amos 5:24.

SATURDAY

Amy Carmichael, *His thoughts said . . . His Father said* (1941).

Martin Marty, *A Cry of Absence* (San Francisco, 1983).

C. Everett Koop, *Sometimes Mountains Move* (Wheaton, IL, 1977).

C. S. Lewis, *The Last Battle* (London, 1956).

George Herbert, "The Flower," from *The Temple*.

Advent Three

SUNDAY

Haggai 2:6.

MONDAY

Carmichael, *His thoughts*.

C. S. Lewis, *Till We Have Faces* (New York, 1957).

TUESDAY

A. M. Allchin, *The World Is a Wedding* (New York, 1978).

The verses of Psalm 45 have been adapted for syntax.

Evelyn Underhill, *Mysticism* (New York, 1961).

Monica Furlong, *Travelling In* (Cambridge, MA, 1984).

Dante, *Purgatory* 6:80–81.

Thomas Aquinas, "Now my tongue."

WEDNESDAY

Gerard Manley Hopkins, "God's Grandeur."

Matthew Fox, "The Case for Extrovert Meditation," *Spirituality Today* (1980).

George A. Maloney, *The Breath of the Mystic* (Denville, NJ, 1974).

C. S. Lewis, *That Hideous Strength* (New York, 1946).

C. S. Lewis, *A Grief Observed* (Greenwich, CT, 1963).

Sister Penelope, *The Wood* (New York, 1973).

THURSDAY

Psalm 50:3.

John Donne, "Holy Sonnets," XIV.

George MacDonald, *The Princess and Curdie* (New York, 1985).

Annie Dillard, *Teaching a Stone to Talk* (New York, 1982).

FRIDAY

C. S. Lewis, *Reflections on the Psalms* (New York, 1958).

Virginia Stem Owens, *And the Trees Clap Their Hands* (Grand Rapids, MI, 1983).

SATURDAY

Owens, *And the Trees Clap Their Hands.*

Advent Four

SUNDAY

Charles Williams, *The Region of the Summer Stars* (London, 1944).

Susan Sontag, *Illness as Metaphor* (New York, 1978).

Joshua Fischman, "Type A on Trial," *Psychology Today* (February 1987).

MONDAY

Isaiah 11:6.

Owen Barfield, *Poetic Diction* (Middletown, CT, 1973).

Austin Farrer, *The Glass of Vision* (London, 1958).

TUESDAY

Charles Williams, *The Image of the City and Other Essays* (London, 1958).

Charles Williams, *All Hallows' Eve* (London, 1945).

Humphrey Carpenter, *The Inklings* (Boston, 1979).

Madison Smartt Bell, *Waiting for the End of the World* (New York, 1985).

WEDNESDAY

Psalm 72:6.

"I Sing of a Maiden," medieval carol.

"There Is No Rose," medieval carol.

THURSDAY

Miles Coverdale, *Fruitful Lessons Upon the Passion*.

Frederick Buechner, *Godric* (New York, 1981).